D0970482

Our Superheroes, Ourselves

Our Superheroes, Ourselves

Edited by Robin S. Rosenberg

OXFORD
UNIVERSITY PRESS

OXFORD
UNIVERSITY PRESS

Oxford University Press is a department of the University of Oxford.
It furthers the University's objective of excellence in research, scholarship,
and education by publishing worldwide.

Oxford New York
Auckland Cape Town Dar es Salaam Hong Kong Karachi
Kuala Lumpur Madrid Melbourne Mexico City Nairobi
New Delhi Shanghai Taipei Toronto

With offices in
Argentina Austria Brazil Chile Czech Republic France Greece
Guatemala Hungary Italy Japan Poland Portugal Singapore
South Korea Switzerland Thailand Turkey Ukraine Vietnam

Oxford is a registered trademark of Oxford University Press in the
UK and certain other countries.

Published in the United States of America by
Oxford University Press
198 Madison Avenue, New York, NY 10016

© Robin Rosenberg 2013

All rights reserved. No part of this publication may be reproduced, stored in a
retrieval system, or transmitted, in any form or by any means, without the prior
permission in writing of Oxford University Press, or as expressly permitted by law,
by license, or under terms agreed with the appropriate reproduction rights organization.
Inquiries concerning reproduction outside the scope of the above should be sent to the
Rights Department, Oxford University Press, at the address above.

You must not circulate this work in any other form
and you must impose this same condition on any acquirer.

Library of Congress Cataloging-in-Publication Data
Our superheroes, ourselves / edited by Robin S. Rosenberg.
p. cm.
Includes bibliographical references and index.
ISBN 978-0-19-976581-2 (acid-free paper) 1. Comic books, strips, etc.—
Psychological aspects. 2. Superheroes—Psychological aspects. 3. Psychology in
literature. 4. Archetype (Psychology) I. Rosenberg, Robin S.
PN6714.O89 2013
741.5′9—dc23 2012035088

1 3 5 7 9 8 6 4 2
Printed in the United States of America
on acid-free paper

To Stephen, with whom anything is possible

Contents

Part II: The Humanity of Superheroes

Acknowledgments

This book, like every book, is a result of teamwork. The teams whose work has led to this book are numerous and varied.

Many thanks to the psychologists who contributed to this book—for being willing to go a bit far afield from the usual type of chapters you write, and for doing it so well. Without you, there would be no book.

Thanks also go to the teams of comic book creators, interpreters, and storytellers, whose stories have intrigued and inspired so many of us.

The team at Oxford University Press deserves thanks both for their interest in publishing not just one book on superheroes, but a series, and for their faith in me to be series editor. Specifically, thanks to editor Abby Gross, and Director of Publicity (and superhero fan) Purdy, as well as Suzanne Walker, Justyna Zajac, Joan Bossert, and Tracy O'Hara.

Thanks to Catherine Carlin Alexander and Angelique Rondeau for their enthusiastic support in the early stages of bringing this book to life.

And of course, thanks to my family. To my brother, Steven, for—among many other things—turning me on to superheroes when I was young. To my mother, Bunny, for supporting me always, in every way. To the other Stephen, for whom there are no words. And to David, Justin, and Neil, who got me interested in superheroes again, and to Rebecca. You are all my team, for which I am grateful.

Contributors

Roy Baumeister
Department of Psychology
Florida State University
Tallahassee, Florida

Elizabeth Behm-Morawitz
Department of
Communication
University of Missouri
Columbia, Missouri

Gary N. Burns
Department of Psychology
Wright State University
Dayton, Ohio

Peter J. Jordan
Griffith Business School
Griffith University
Nathan, Australia

Travis Langley
Department of Psychology
Henderson State University
Arkadelphia, Arkansas

Mikhail Lyubansky
Department of Psychology
University of Illinois at
Urbana-Champaign
Urbana, Illinois

Megan B. Morris
Department of Psychology
Wright State University
Dayton, Ohio

Hillary Pennell
Department of Communication
University of Missouri
Columbia, Missouri

David A. Pizarro
Department of Psychology
Cornell University
Ithaca, New York

Robin S. Rosenberg
Department of Psychiatry
University of California
San Francisco, California

Lawrence C. Rubin
Department of Social Sciences and Counseling
St. Thomas University
Miami, Florida

Robert J. Sternberg
Department of Psychology
Oklahoma State University
Stillwater, Oklahoma

Ellen Winner
Department of Psychology
Boston College
Boston, Massachusetts

Introduction

Robin S. Rosenberg

You'd have to live in a cave to escape the current superhero craze. Most people—from hardcore superhero fans to those with a less passionate interest—find themselves wondering about superheroes' crossover into mainstream culture. "Why are superheroes so popular?" we ask. We wonder what the popularity of superheroes says about us as a society. In essence, this curiosity is about *our relationship with superheroes*.

Beyond this meta-awareness of superheroes' impact on our culture, even casual fans of superheroes are intrigued by some of the issues raised in superhero stories—issues of morality and justice, of personality and identity. As with any good fiction that endures, we resonate with the superhero characters, and their stories spark our imaginations. The power of these stories entices each of us to wonder: What would I do if I were in the superhero's position? How realistic are the superheroes' actions? What might it be like to live in their world or have their powers? In essence, these questions reflect a curiosity about superheroes *as if superheroes were real*. How they are similar to and different from us.

Both sets of issues ultimately are about psychological matters that relate superheroes to ourselves. Who better to discuss such psychological matters than psychologists? That's the idea behind this book, which is a collection of essays by noted psychologists in which the authors apply their knowledge of psychology to our relationship with superheroes, and the extent to which superheroes' psychological nature reflects human nature.

These two issues about superheroes are also reflected in the two meanings of the title of this book, *Our Superheroes, Ourselves*. One meaning is captured by the title of the first section of essays: "Our Relationship with Superheroes." These essays focus on:

- our fascination with superheroes (by Robin Rosenberg);
- our fascination with supervillains and their immorality (by David Pizarro and Roy Baumeister);
- the question of whether superhero stories are good for people (by Lawrence Rubin);
- the power of superheroes' emotional lives and why readers resonate (by Peter Jordan);
- how superheroes' bodies can influence our view of our own bodies (by Hillary Pennell and Elizabeth Behm-Morawitz).

The other meaning of the book title is about the comparison between superheroes and ourselves. In a way, superheroes serve as (funhouse) mirrors through which we catch our own images—sometimes exaggerated and distorted, sometimes not. When superhero stories lead us to ask ourselves "how would I handle that situation?" or "what would it be like to have a power?" what we're doing is comparing ourselves to superheroes and trying to figure out how similar to and different from them we are, and whether superhero stories can teach us something about ourselves. (Yes, I know that superhero comics, television shows, and films are entertaining, but their phenomenal popularity suggests that there is more going on than simply entertainment.)

In fact, we can learn about ourselves when we compare ourselves to superheroes, especially when we focus on psychological attributes. Because most superheroes—even the ones who aren't human—function psychologically as humans. Superman may be from Krypton, but his childhood struggles with being gifted aren't that different from the struggles of gifted children in our world (and the differences between his struggles and that of people in our world are illuminating—see Chapter 7). Superhero stories were written, drawn, directed, and acted by humans (in so far as we know) and so the stories—especially the powerful stories—reflect their creators' knowledge and assumptions about people and about human nature. The essays in second section of the book, "The Humanity of Superheroes," address this psychological comparison. These essays include:

- How people's views of superheroes' and supervillains' personalities contrast with their view of their own personalities (by Travis Langley);
- How superheroes' powers and abilities—which make them *gifted*—compare with being gifted in our world (by Robin Rosenberg and Ellen Winner);
- The extent to which superheroes' work lives mirror what we know about our work lives (by Gary Burns and Megan B. Morris);
- The wisdom and ethics of superheroes and what we can learn from them (by Robert Sternberg);
- Justice in superheroes' worlds and our world (by Mikhail Lyubansky).

As you'll see from the essays, the authors have brought to bear their psychological expertise and applied it to superheroes and to us. Hopefully the essays will intrigue you as well as teach you something about yourself, if not about superheroes.

Enjoy!

Robin S. Rosenberg
San Francisco, CA

Our Superheroes, Ourselves

PART I

Our Relationship with Superheroes

ONE

Our Fascination with Superheroes

Robin S. Rosenberg

EDITOR'S NOTE

Superhero films keep being made and superhero stories keep being written because many people enjoy good superhero stories. In this essay, I draw on my knowledge of psychology and my research with superhero fans to explore why we are fascinated by superheroes—why their appeal is about more than good action stories or escapism.

—Robin S. Rosenberg

If you're reading this, it's probably because you have at least a passing interest in superheroes. You're not alone. Perhaps your interest in superheroes dates back to your youth, reading comic books or watching Saturday morning cartoons. Or maybe you watched a superhero movie or television show. In any case, there was something about superheroes—or a particular superhero—that piqued your interest and got you thinking or fantasizing. What is it about superheroes and their stories that captivates or intrigues us? Is it the underlying morality tales, the familiarity of the story arcs, the appealing characters, or the action? Different elements appeal to each individual. See whether any of the reasons I discuss below resonate with you.

A CALLBACK TO YOUTH

An adult experience with superheroes can remind us of our childhood: the ways that our imagination was so powerful that our fantasies seemed real. I think that superhero stories, particularly films that have good special effects, a good script, and well-acted characters, create a bridge between our childhood fantasies and our adult realism. Consider that children are more hypnotizable than adults,[1] and can more readily and vividly go into their own world, shutting out external reality and creating a world limited only by their imagination. Live-action superhero stories allow us to recapture periods of our childhood when our imaginations were cranked up to the maximum—when we really *believed* we could fly or knock down the bad guy or save the city from disaster.

I suggest that superhero films in a darkened movie theater are most able to put us into this fantasied land. The darkened theater minimizes the viewer's visual awareness of anything other than the screen. It's easier to lose track of the person sitting in the next seat or the kids fidgeting a few rows ahead. We could turn the lights down at home when watching a DVD or television show, but unless the screen at home is a very large one, a movie theater viewing experience is still likely to be better because the screen fills the viewer's visual field. All these visual elements (and of course the surround sound) make it easier to immerse ourselves in the film. And with a superhero film, we are immersing ourselves in a fantasied world. As in the *Toy Story* films, previously static figures (in this case, of comic book characters) come to life before our very eyes.

SUPERHEROES ARE FAMILIAR AND COMFORTING

Superhero stories are familiar. The superhero is challenged by a moral dilemma, physical trial, or both (often instigated by a villain). The superhero triumphs, sometimes learning and growing in the process. Spider-Man must defeat the Green Goblin, and in doing so discovers his own strength of character. The Joker induces Batman to make difficult choices (such as choosing whether to rescue Harvey Dent or Rachel Dawes, in *The Dark Knight*) and in doing so Batman learns something about his opponent and himself.

The stories generally follow the standard basic plots with which we are familiar.[2] In fact, we may know the form of the story arc even before the story begins. This is especially true of origin stories, which form the bread and butter of superhero films and typically conform to some version of the hero's journey in which the protagonist is, after some challenges and setbacks, transformed and dedicates his or her life to an altruistic purpose.[3] After all, that's what hero stories are about. In this way, the stories are, broadly speaking, predictable and formulaic.

Being formulaic isn't necessarily a bad thing. Research on readers' enjoyment of a related type of story—mysteries—indicates that people generally enjoy simpler stories more than complex ones.[4] We may prefer our superhero stories to be relatively simple. Their predictable, formulaic tales can also be reassuring: We can allow ourselves to become anxious on behalf of the story's characters because we know that all will turn out right in the end. Or if not at the end of one episode or comic book story, then in a subsequent one. (I am making a general statement. In comic books, some superheroes or their sidekicks have had long-term or seemingly permanent harm befall them, as when Superman dies in the *Death of Superhero* [1992], Batgirl becomes permanently paralyzed in *The Killing Joke* [1988], or when Captain America dies in *The Death of Captain America* [2007–2008]. These instances stand out because they do not follow the conventional pattern of the superhero always triumphing. William Goldman's wonderful novel *The Princess Bride* and the film version of his book play on the reader/viewer's expectations of the hero triumphing in the end.)

A story's tension is thus cathartic.[5] We don't have to worry about getting too devastated, as we might with more realistic hero stories that don't have a formulaic plot. In fact, *The Dark Knight* film took many of viewers by surprise *because* a main character dies. **[Spoiler alert!]** If you're like most viewers of that film, you probably thought that both Harvey Dent and Rachel Dawes would be saved simultaneously. Similarly, *Star Trek* prequel viewers were likely surprised when Spock's mother dies because we know from previous *Star Trek* stories that she's supposed to live! Our complacency about predicting a happy ending was challenged in these films. This was also true toward the end of the film *The Dark Knight Rises*.

SUPERHEROES AS A SPECIAL KIND OF ESCAPE

Good fiction, and good storytelling of any kind, allows us to become immersed in someone else's world and in doing so provides us with both an escape and emotional engagement.[6] We can lose ourselves and temporarily forget our worries and woes, fears and foes. We also get drawn in to the characters' world and issues. Superheroes stories, even when stories take place on alien worlds—such as Green Lantern's Oa or Thor's Asgard—provide human dilemmas in different contexts, as did Greek myths and other enduring mythic tales. The stories' core themes of right versus wrong, personal choice, sacrifice for the greater good, finding purpose and meaning, resonate with readers and viewers. The way these themes play out in superhero stories can get us feeling and thinking,[7] as the stories explore potential dire consequences as a result of particular actions. A 1970 Green Arrow/Green Lantern story (issue #81),[8] for instance, was ahead of its time, exploring the theme of overpopulation; the two superheroes visit the planet Maltus and see the dire effects of overpopulation, yet there is no "villain" behind it. A life-and-death version of game theory is explored in the film *The*

Dark Knight (2008), when the Joker rigs two ships to blow up, with each ship holding the detonator to and fate of the other ship.[9]

Superhero stories also highlight current political issues by exaggerating them, providing moral and political commentary. X-Men stories in comics and film, for example, explore themes of prejudice and discrimination as well as institutionally sanctioned discrimination, such as state-sponsored kidnapping and experimentation on mutants. (Among the X-Men films, these issues stand out in *X-Men 2*, released in 2003.)

Above all, the stories provide drama, action, suspense, and romance. They present us with action, aggression, villains we love to hate, moral dilemmas, and protagonists who inspire us. There's something for most everyone, and always a different world into which we can, at minimum, escape for a while.

ROOTING FOR A DIFFERENT KIND OF HOME TEAM

Superhero stories can tug at us the same way that local sports teams do—they give us a way to root for the home team unabashedly and without reserve. There aren't that many nonsport opportunities in which large swatches of society can be on the same side. Political parties and events often leave us divided, but superhero stories allow us to come together nationally and even internationally and all be on the same team—the superhero's team.

We seem to love to have heroes, and superheroes are not likely to let us down the way real teams or real heroes do. We elevate sports figures or politicians as heroes, but in doing so, we make them both more than human and less than human. We don't allow them to be actual humans. We raise them up and want them to be better than we are, to be flawless. It seems to me that we don't want to recognize that real heroes in our world are people, with strengths and weakness, great courage, and often significant foibles or even vices. When we get a glimpse of their human side—their marital problems, substance use, financial troubles—we push them off their pedestals. They are heroes no longer.[10]

In this way we seem to propel our heroes onto a ridiculous roller coaster: We raise them up and imbue them with (or project onto them) attributes that are far in excess of their heroic actions. And when we find out they're only human—when we discover their "underside," their negative qualities—we demonize them. We push them from the heights of the rollercoaster to its depths. They—and we—scream and cry as they make their descent. We're disappointed in them, yet in most cases they never claimed to be more than they actually were. When we find out that they've got an unheroic underside we are surprised, though we shouldn't be. We may feel betrayed, but we shouldn't. Someone can be a hero in one context and be an awful person, or just an average person, in another context. These complex and nuanced aspects of our real heroes can leave us feeling unfulfilled, akin to eating a large bucket of popcorn: our bellies are full but we still crave something to eat.

Superhero stories can make us feel satisfied, like we've had a meal. We can applaud superheroes without reserve because even if they have an underside, we seem to allow them to have character flaws in a way that we don't necessary allow our real heroes. In fact, whereas flaws in our real life heroes serve to tarnish them, flaws in superheroes add character and depth. Green Lantern helps out those on other planets but doesn't help fix social ills on our own planet. Yet we don't hold it against him. Similarly, Superman saves kittens from trees but allows people to starve. Iron Man and Green Arrow are both full of themselves and horrendous womanizers, often cheating on their girlfriends (or wife in Green Arrow's case). Wolverine is impulsive and prone to anger, but we forgive him. Iron Man goes through a period of alcoholism. We allow superheroes their humanity in a way that we don't allow real heroes. As Carroll wrote, "the contemporary hero [exists] in an instant-media-driven society in which we seek to raise people to impossible heights and then inevitably wait for the fall."[11] Superheroes don't fall—at least not permanently. This is part of the unspoken promise of superhero stories.

FROM MORE PSYCHOLOGICALLY COMPLEX STORIES, EXISTENTIAL CRISES

Until the dawn of the 1980s, superheroes weren't generally part of the adult mainstream. Kids had a slew of Saturday morning superhero cartoon and comic books. Occasional family-centered live-action superhero stories graced the small screen: Superman in the 1950s, Batman and Robin in the 1960s, and Wonder Woman in the 1970s. Then superheroes came to film: Christopher Reeve's Superman films in the 1970s and 1980s and the Batman films in the 1980s and 1990s. (Note that *Superman I* wasn't the first superhero film. Among earlier releases was *Batman: The Movie*—a film extension of the Batman television series—released in 1966. The Superman film, though, was the first superhero feature film specifically aimed for a general audience. No prior superhero familiarity needed. Other superhero films released in the 1980s and 1990s didn't make the same splash, such as *Supergirl* [1984] and *The Phantom* [1996]). While Christopher Reeve's Superman and Tim Burton's Batman were captivating mainstream audiences, superhero comics with darker themes—for adults—were published, such as Alan Moore's *The Watchmen* (1986–1987) and *The Killing Joke* (1988), and Frank Miller's *The Dark Knight Returns* (1986).

As writers have aimed their stories at adults, the plots have become more complex, and superheroes have become more three-dimensional and prone to existential crises, often provoked by the increased sadism and violence in their villains. They come to struggle with the issues with which we struggle. In this sense, they've become more like us.

Granted, Marvel superheroes have always been more "human" and relatable, with everyday problems such as financial troubles (Spider-Man), family squabbles (Fantastic Four, Thor), relationship issues (Spider-Man, Iron Man, Daredevil, to name a few), work issues (The Avengers), assimilation issues (Thor), and even alcoholism (Iron Man). DC may have come late to having their superheroes struggle with real issues, but their superheroes do: drug abuse (Speedy, Green Arrow's sidekick), prostitution and HIV infection (Mia Deardon, before she became Green Arrow's subsequent Speedy), philandering (Green Arrow), the desire for official recognition (Wonder Woman), loss and guilt (Batman), and dealing with losing the respect of others (Superman). Nonetheless, the psychological nuance to the characters seems to have increased over the decades.

As our problems have become their problems, we are fascinated to see how the issues play out in the funhouse mirror of superheroes' worlds. In Superman stories, for instance, we get to see the consequences of electing a megalomaniac for president (Lex Luthor). In Batman stories we see how he handles grief and guilt after the murder of the second Robin, Jason Todd. (In the story "A Death in the Family" [*Batman #426–429*, 1988–1989], the Joker beats Jason Todd mercilessly, ties him up and sets a bomb to go off. Todd dies soon after the bomb explodes. A version of this story is recounted in the DVD movie *Under the Red Hood* [2010].)

In X-Men stories we see how racism and discrimination harm both the group doing the discriminating as well as those on the receiving end. Spider-Man shows us the personal cost of spending all your time helping others.

Superhero stories also present us with moral dilemmas. Batman, Superman, Spider-Man, and other superheroes have villains who create the horrible but classic dilemma of forcing the hero to choose whom to save: a loved one or a group of innocents about to be killed by the villain. Although most of us, fortunately, won't have to face this dilemma ourselves, in watching our superheroes struggle with this no-win conundrum, many of us ask ourselves "what would I do if faced with this horrible choice?" Moreover, since the 1980s, the villains in superhero stories have become increasingly twisted and sadistic—think of recent versions of the Joker—at least in the stories targeted at adults, putting our superheroes in even more intense and challenging situations. In turn, Batman stories targeted to adults repeatedly challenge the reader or viewer to entertain the question of why Batman doesn't just kill the Joker, given all the innocent lives that will likely be saved in the future were the Joker to exist no longer. Such stories can induce us to wrestle with issues about justice, the death penalty, and the question of rehabilitation for certain types of criminals, among other issues.

Here's another effect of the more psychologically complex stories: when we identify with the character, we may experience more emotions while watching or reading the story. Research on stories that are written with the use of first-person narration suggests that this literary device leads people to experience more emotion in response to the story.[12] In fact, superhero comic book stories have included first-person narration for decades in the form of thought bubbles and, more recently, with the shift in the narrator from an anonymous third-person to the first-person of the superhero. It makes it easier to put ourselves in their shoes.

A SUPERHERO FOR EVERYONE

Superheroes are not monolithic. Like us, each superhero has his or her own unique constellation of personality traits, abilities and vulnerabilities, desires and demons. In turn, a superhero's character is nudged in one direction or another by each writer. Some superheroes are not even conventional heroes; they are "antiheroes" who fight crime for selfish, not altruistic, reasons that involve revenge. The Punisher, a vigilante, is an example; his wife and children, who witnessed a Mafia hit, were then killed. He vowed revenge on the mob and all criminals.

In general, superheroes are alike in some key ways: they each have at least one enhanced ability, they each are committed to doing "good" in some way that involves physical battles, and they each wear a costume or uniform. (A notable exception: The DC superhero Batgirl [Barbara Gordon] was paralyzed by the Joker in *The Killing Joke*, and for decades had been wheelchair-bound and so did not engage in physical battles nor wear a uniform. She worked behind the scenes. When DC relaunched their universe in 2011, Barbara Gordon became fully mobile as Batgirl, despite protests from fans about the change.)

A Personality for Everyone

Just as we are drawn to some people because of their personality, we are drawn to some superheroes but not others. We identify or aspire to be like some and not others. When I am at a comic convention, I walk through the exhibit halls, interviewing attendees. Among other questions, I ask them who their favorite superheroes are and why. Some people say that Batman is their favorite, but their reasons vary. Some identify with his traumatic history from childhood, others take comfort from the way he has made meaning of his adversity ("if he can pull through and help others, it inspires me to do the same"). Some Wonder Woman fans aspire to be like her—confident with herself and her body. Still others identify with Spider-Man, who juggles multiple real life problems, fights crime, and tries to do the right thing in all spheres of his life.

The Coolest Power

Superheroes don't all have the same powers (except perhaps for persistence in the face of adversity). We can be drawn to or fascinated by a given superhero because we are captivated by his or her power or ability. We may wonder what it would be like to fly, or how we might use a spider-sense. Or we may be awed by the human superheroes, who use their human talents to maximal advantage. Whatever our favorite power or ability, the idea of it gets us thinking about how it could be used. Superhero stories offer us models.

Resonating with Superhero Themes: Dual Identity and Being Different

Most of us can resonate with at least two aspects of the dual identity of many superheroes: that we are different people in different contexts (how we are with a romantic partner may be very different from how we are when relating to a boss) and that in our daily lives we feel that people don't accurately see our real selves and all of our potential. In the film *Batman Begins* (2005), Bruce Wayne tries to convey to Rachel Dawes that he is more than the playboy he appears to be: "all of this [referring to the women and his opulent lifestyle]... it's not me... inside. I am... I am more." Just as people look at Bruce Wayne and see a rich playboy (though he is anything but a playboy), we too may feel that people see only a superficial persona. But we know that there is more to us than meets the eye.

Another theme in superhero stories with which many can identify is that of *being different*. In such contexts, different means "not good," even for superpowered Superman, who struggles to find a comfortable way to live as an alien among humans. To be different and not feel alone. The theme of being different is perhaps most prominent in X-Men stories, in which we learn that many mutants were made fun of, harassed, or nearly killed because of their abilities. Like Superman, Marvel's mutants learned at a young age to hide their abilities. It is only at Professor Xavier's School for Gifted Children that the mutants are able to feel truly comfortable with themselves because they are with people who are also different. This relief at finding other "different" people is portrayed in the film *X-Men: First Class*, when the young mutants sit around showing each other their powers and are applauded rather than ridiculed. In our world, people can feel the same relief at finding a group of like-minded but "different" folks in college (perhaps through activity groups that share the same interest, such as an anime club) or in online chat rooms or forums. Interests or problems that we'd been hiding from others can at last be shared with folks in a similar boat. What a relief!

INSPIRATION

Superheroes inspire us. They are engaged in a never-ending fight against crime and villainy. They fight the good fight even when they're tired, burned out, or have crises in their personal lives. When it's hard to know what the "right decision" is, they generally don't get flummoxed. They are decisive. In these ways, they are like real soldiers. Their exploits and dedication are inspiring. Moreover, they have a clarity of purpose, and a moral compass that is usually enviable, even if we don't agree with the specifics.

From time to time they have existential crises and question whether all their efforts and sacrifices are worth it. This happens to Superman in the graphic novel *Kingdom Come* (1996), Peter Parker in various comics and in the film *Spider-Man 2* (2004), and Batman in the film *The Dark Knight* (2008) and in the Batman graphic novel by Kevin Smith *The Widening Gyre* (2009–2010). When the superheroes come out the other side of their crises, they come back to their superhero work with renewed dedication.

A WISH FOR A RESCUER

Superhero stories call us back to our youth, to a time when right and wrong seemed simpler and easier to discern. Many children's stories are filled with heroes who save the day. Such stories reflect a common wish or fantasy that when bad things happen or are about to happen, someone comes to help. Superhero stories tap into this wish. Superheroes protect the defenseless, round up criminals and evildoers, and put themselves on the line for others. As children, we both wanted someone to do that for us and wanted to be the superhero.

Superhero stories may have been around for decades, but the characters and stories picked up steam in the adult mainstream in the new millennium. Why the sudden explosion of superheroes everywhere, and our fascination with them? A confluence of events may have played a large part. First, the events of September 11, 2001 (and the anthrax scare days afterward). This event—the first such major tragedy on American soil essentially unfolding live on the Internet and television—led Americans as well as people in other countries to feel more vulnerable. Common reactions, aside from horror, anger, and sadness, were "this could happen anywhere," "this could happen to me," and "is there no way to stop this?" In a sense, we all became terror's victims.

Collectively, we began to yearn for larger-than-life heroes—to be inspired by them and to be rescued by them. Coincidentally, within a year of 9/11, the first *Spider-Man* film was released; it did fantastically at the box office. Similarly, the television shows *24* and *Smallville* (about Superman during high school years) launched to commercial success. (Although *24*'s Jack Bauer isn't technically a superhero, the show portrays him acting heroically, and he seems to have some "super" abilities, including his ability to tolerate and inflict pain.) Superhero stories thus provide us with a fantasied rescuer at a time when we, as a society, really want one.

POWER OF THE MEDIA TO PERSUADE

Here's one final reason why I think we're fascinated by superheroes: They are everywhere. On screens big and small, on billboards and buses, on lunchboxes and T-shirts. Hollywood studios invest heavily in superhero films (after all, it costs a lot of money to make the CGI scenes live up to our imagination). They advertise so heavily that it's hard to avoid being exposed to superhero films. This blanket of advertising and merchandising provides a *mere exposure effect*, in which by becoming familiar with something, we come to change our attitude toward it, generally in the positive direction.[13] People see ads for the superhero films, and if they weren't already inclined toward superheroes, they become at least somewhat curious to see what "all the fuss" is about, unless they are resolutely not interested in superheroes. If the film's story and character development are good, it seals the deal, accounting for the phenomenal popularity of the *Batman* films (the Christopher Nolan films as well as the Tim Burton ones), the *Iron Man* films, the *Avenger* film, and the *Spider-Man* films.

CONCLUSION

Superheroes can be fascinating for a multitude of reasons: they provide escape, their familiar storylines are comforting, they provide us with a person or team to cheer on, they allow us to see issues, existential crises, and our own problems in displacement. Moreover, the variety of superheroes—of powers, of personality, of personal dilemmas—lets our fascination fall on the superheroes who are the best "match" for us.

Superheroes—in contrast to heroes or other protagonists—are simultaneously like us and not like us. Their superpowers can make us fantasize what it would be like to be them, while at the same time wishing there were *someone* who was like them in real life.

NOTES

1. Ward, C. (1994). Culture and altered states of consciousness. In W. J. Lonner & R. S. Malpass (Eds.), *Psychology and culture* (pp. 59–64). Boston: Allyn and Bacon.
2. Booker, C. (2004). *The seven basic plots: Why we tell stories.* New York: Continuum.
3. Campbell, J. (2008). *The hero with a thousand faces.* New York: New World Library.
4. Knobloch-Westerwick, S., & Keplinger, C. (2008). Murder for pleasure: Impacts of plot complexity and need for cognition on mystery enjoyment. *Journal of Media Psychology: Theories, Methods, and Applications*, *20*(3), 117–128.
5. Zillmann, D. (2000). Humor and comedy. In D. Zillmann & P. Vorderer (Eds.), *Media entertainment: The psychology of its appeal* (pp. 59–72). Mahwah, NJ: Erlbaum.
6. Mar, R. A., Oatley, K., Djikic, M., & Mullin, J. (2011). Emotion and narrative fiction: Interactive influences before, during, and after reading. *Cognition and Emotion*, *25*(5), 818–833.

7. Sriraman, B., & Adrian, H. (1999). The use of fiction as a didactic tool to examine existential problems. *Journal of Secondary Gifted Education*, *10*(3), 96–106.
8. Story by Dennis O'Neil and art by Neal Adams.
9. For more on the specifics of the game theory of this part of the film, go to http://www.quantitativepeace.com/blog/2008/07/the-dark-knight.html.
10. Carroll, L. (2011). America's hero problem. *The Atlantic*. September 7. Accessed on December 18, 2011, at http://www.theatlantic.com/entertainment/print/2011/09/americas-hero-problem/244659/
11. Carroll, (2011).
12. Gholamain, M. (1998). *The attachment and personality dynamics of reader response*. Toronto: National Library of Canada.
13. Zajonc, R. B. (1968). Attitudinal effects of mere exposure. *Journal of Personality and Social Psychology*, 9(2, Pt. 2), 1–27.

TWO

Superhero Comics as Moral Pornography

David A. Pizarro and Roy Baumeister

Editor's Note

Superheroes aren't the only "super" people we're fascinated by. We're also fascinated by supervillains. To understand this fascination, David Pizarro and Roy Baumeister apply psychological research from a variety of areas including the appeal of pornography, moral judgments and decision-making, and why "evil" is perpetrated. Pizarro and Baumeister are a perfect duo to discuss this topic; their research includes work on moral judgments, aggression, and self-defeating behaviors.

—Robin S. Rosenberg

Stories about good and evil are among the oldest stories told. These moral tales often describe a hero who struggles against the forces of evil in its various guises. In these stories, evil is often personified as an enemy for the hero to overcome. For instance, in the oldest work of literature known to exist, the Mesopotamian hero Gilgamesh battles a giant who has the face of a lion and whose "roar is a flood, his mouth is death, and his breath is fire."[1]

Modern superhero comics (and the films they've inspired) are moral tales on steroids. While they present variations on the theme of good versus evil, these stories describe individuals who commit moral deeds of global (and often cosmic) significance on a weekly basis. In this chapter we will argue that superhero comics, like other moralistic tales, are popular in part because they satisfy a basic human motivation: the motivation to divide the social world into good people and bad, and to morally praise and condemn them accordingly. In their modern superhero comic incarnation, however, these tales depict an exaggerated morality that has been stripped of its real-world subtlety. In tales of superhero versus supervillain, moral good and moral bad are always the actions of easily identifiable moral agents with unambiguous intentions and actions. It is these very qualities that make these stories so enjoyable. Much like the appeal of the exaggerated, caricatured sexuality found in pornography, superhero comics offer the appeal of an exaggerated and caricatured morality that satisfies the natural human inclination toward moralization. In short, the modern superhero comic is a form of "moral pornography"—built to satisfy our moralistic urges, but ultimately unrealistic and, in the end, potentially misleading.

THE PARADOXICAL POPULARITY OF THE SUPERVILLAIN

Some things are so obvious that they require little explanation. Take the popularity of Superman: why *wouldn't* people want to have an invulnerable superhero on their side (let alone one who fights for truth and justice, saves lives in his spare time, and is a genuinely nice guy)? Perhaps the popularity of Superman seems obvious because heroic characters with superhuman abilities are so old and familiar. Or perhaps superheroes are so popular because they are a straightforward extension of "regular" heroes—who wouldn't like a "super" hero, capable of doing so much more than a normal one?

But the emergence of the comic book superhero gave rise to something a bit harder to explain—the unexpected popularity of the *supervillain.* This popularity is perplexing given what we know about human morality. After all, most individuals are not fond of immoral people, nor do they take pleasure in hearing about morally heinous acts. If anything, individuals actively avoid others with whom they disagree in the moral domain.[2] Yet supervillains—who, by definition, are orders of magnitude more evil than any ordinary evildoer—are treated with fascination, curiosity, and delight. The extent of their moral depravity seems linked to their popularity: In 2009, when the website IGN.com ranked the top comic book characters of all time, they began by publishing a list of top villains.[3] Only a year later did they publish the equivalent list of superheroes. Occupying the top positions were two of the most brutal characters in the history of comics: the Joker (a psychopathic, indiscriminate killer, who despite lacking any special powers has a body count that is among the highest of all comic book villains), and Magneto (the archenemy of the X-Men, his disdain for the entire human race is responsible for the deaths of thousands). These supervillains are not just popular among people who visit websites about comics and attend comic conventions, either: the films that feature these villains (such as *The Dark Knight*) are among the most popular and highest grossing films of all time.[4] Why would people take such delight in following the stories of these monstrous characters (whose closest real-world analogs are individuals like Adolf Hitler and Pol Pot), let alone put their likeness on movie posters and on their children's lunchboxes?

Perhaps supervillains are popular because superheroes, by themselves, are boring. A simple thought experiment illustrates this: imagine a world, like ours, where bad guys do bad things and good guys try to stop them. What would *really* happen if someone with superhuman abilities (someone who had superhuman strength, the ability to control minds, or who could run at the speed of sound) were to suddenly appear? If this person chose to dedicate himself to preventing crime, regular criminals would stand little chance, crime would dwindle, and the story would be over. By introducing a powerful foe who can repeatedly test the hero's mettle, however, the story remains interesting. Comic books are hardly the first instance of this phenomenon. Milton's *Paradise Lost* was intended as a religiously inspiring poem, but the consensus among critics over the centuries has been that the devil is the most interesting character, and the one with the best lines.[5]

Supervillains serve as foils to keep the superheroes motivated. But while their convenience as a literary device may account for their regular presence in superhero comics, it cannot explain the degree of popularity they enjoy.

THE POWER OF BAD

The fascinating appeal of supervillains is consistent with an important principle of psychology: Bad is stronger than good. A review article[6] examined dozens of findings and concluded that bad actions, events, emotions, and experiences routinely have greater psychological impact than good ones. Indeed, it was hard to find any exceptions to this principle. One recent source of evidence illustrates the psychological power of bad: while thinking about ourselves as moral agents can make us physically stronger, this effect is stronger when we imagine ourselves as committing acts of evil rather than good.[7]

To be sure, life is generally good in peaceful, modern societies. But that is because there are far *more* good things than bad. Successful marriages, for instance, are characterized by the presence of at least five good interactions for every bad one—the so-called Gottman Ratio.[8] Applying this ratio—five units of "good" required for every one unit of "bad"—to the universe of comic books would mean that for "good" to prevail, it would require presence of about five or six superheroes for every supervillain (of course, we are speaking about villains of the "super" sort, not those of the everyday variety). That might be more realistic, but it would hardly make for thrilling reading. Readers like to see the lone superhero defeating swarms of bad guys.

In that connection, it is instructive to compare fiction against reality. One of the biggest news stories of the year 2011 was the killing of Osama bin Laden by a team of American soldiers. It is relevant that a large team was used, as opposed to sending in a lone assassin who would outshoot the hordes of defenders. In comics (and films) one would have most likely seen a lone hero defeating a large number of bad guys. But in the real world, the good guys manage to win by outnumbering their enemies.

Thus, the high success rate of superheroes in defeating supervillains, in issue after issue of comic book after comic book, is wildly implausible. Moreover, even if their powers were evenly matched, the heroes would be constrained by scruples (not initiating the fight, not killing) and concerns (not endangering innocent bystanders) that would not deter the villains. In reality, a 40 percent victory rate by superheroes would be impressive. In the comics, however, the good guys win almost every time. Comic books provide a satisfying escape—by giving us a universe in which good is stronger than bad.

This is one sense in which the term "moral pornography" is an apt description of comic book morality—it is characterized by an unrealistically high rate of desired outcomes. Consumers of pornography are mostly young and middle-aged men, whose lives are often characterized by getting much less sex than they desire.[9] To get even a small part of the sex they would like to have, they have to make many attempts and endure many rejections. But in pornography, the odds are quite different. In these depictions, most of the women are eager and willing, and the desired outcome—great sex—is almost always obtained by the men who seek it (an unlikely occurrence for most young men in real life). Similarly, the rate of the desired outcome—success against the villain—is unrealistically lopsided in the world of superhero comics, where heroes almost always win the battle against the supervillains.

MORAL SHADOWBOXING

Another explanation for the popularity of supervillains is that they provide people with the ability to exercise their moral faculties—to identify the bad guy, know why he does what he does, and condemn his actions. Taking part in this mock moral judgment appears to be intrinsically enjoyable. Yet while comic book supervillains might be easier to spot (even if you are unfamiliar with comic books, you probably wouldn't invite a guy wearing a metal mask and calling himself "Dr. Doom" on your family vacation), people have been deriving pleasure from jeering fictional villains for quite some time. It was not uncommon, for instance, for moviegoing audiences of the past to boo and hiss loudly whenever the villain appeared onscreen. Early filmmakers did their part to facilitate this behavior by providing obvious cues for audiences to identify the villain. Even before committing his villainous deeds, the villain could be seen twirling his mustache, cackling, and rubbing his hands together, often as the background music gave way to more menacing notes.[10] In Westerns, a similar custom emerged: black hats and white hats marked the bad cowboy and good cowboy, respectively. Even in modern films, telling the heroes apart from the villains is much easier than doing so in real life (Darth Vader, arguably the most famous movie villain in cinematic history, is also one of the most recognizably evil).

Serious literature went through a similar development. In medieval theater, evil was represented by characters who were named or physically labeled with their vices. There was no mistaking them. But during the early modern period (1500–1800), theater came to feature villains in a new sense. These were characters who were soon recognized by the audience as evil but not by the other characters in the play. Often much of the suspense of the play was based on whether the protagonists would discover the wicked schemes and actions of the villains before it was too late.[11] Later, such overtly wicked characters were dismissed from serious literature as not being sufficiently realistic. But their perennial popularity in comic books is indicative of the appeal of moral clarity.

But this is only part of the story—what needs explaining is *why* people seem to get such pleasure from engaging in the moral exercise of identifying and jeering the bad guys. This is where recent psychological research can shed light: individuals likely find this behavior pleasurable because it turns out to be good for them.

WHY MORALITY?

In order to understand why people seem to enjoy judging and hating supervillains, it helps to understand a bit more about the nature of human morality. It is increasingly evident that morality is deeply ingrained in human psychology. It was once believed, however, that human morality was only a result of acculturation and an ability individuals possess to override humanity's basic, immoral nature. This view was thought to be consistent with the theory of natural selection, which appeared to have little room for morality, but that portrayed human beings as survival machines driven by egoistic interests. This is no longer a very popular view. Research from a wide variety of disciplines, spanning from evolutionary biology to social psychology, is converging on the view that human morality is, in fact, consistent with what scientists know about evolution by natural selection: Evolution may have favored individuals who had basic moral intuitions and motivations, such as a desire to act cooperatively and altruistically.[12]

For instance, researchers believe that human altruism likely emerged as a result of two evolutionary mechanisms: *kin selection* (a willingness to act altruistically toward members of one's immediate gene pool) and *reciprocal altruism* (a willingness to act for the benefit of others when there is a chance that the organism will be paid in kind). Together, these mechanisms would have encouraged altruistic behavior, likely by giving rise to the presence of certain moral emotions, such as empathy for the suffering of others or anger over being cheated.[13] The understanding that morality is consistent with the process of evolution represented a large step toward understanding the nature of human morality. In particular, it paved the way toward conceptualizing just how fundamental morality is to human psychology.

A great deal of research from the fields of social psychology, developmental psychology, and social/cognitive neuroscience is providing additional evidence that humans are, in some ways, "hardwired" to be ethical creatures. Obviously, this does not mean that genes drive people to engage in ethically impeccable behavior, but only that people are innately prepared to learn to make and understand moral judgments.

For instance, there is a great deal of evidence that individuals have a basic and strong aversion to being treated unfairly. In studies that investigate fairness in a laboratory setting by having individuals participate in an economic game in which they are asked to engage in a financial exchange with a partner, one of the most reliable findings is the strength of people's reactions to being treated in a way they perceive to be unfair—so much so that they are willing to incur a financial cost just to punish the unfair agent. People enjoy being treated fairly, and become distressed when treated unfairly. While decades of behavioral research support this conclusion, recent research has demonstrated this at a neurological level: areas of the brain associated with pleasure and reward are active when individuals receive fair treatment, and areas of the brain associated with pain and distress are active when they are treated unfairly.[14] In short, we experience pain and pleasure as a reaction to the moral behavior of others.

Another feature of morality that seems to be deeply entrenched in human psychology is the motivation to evaluate others morally. This makes sense, as few tasks are as important as figuring out who the good guys and the bad guys are in everyday life. Being skilled at distinguishing a potential friend from a potential foe likely provided a clear benefit for the survival, reproduction, and social success of an individual who lived in a socially complex environment.[15] Having the ability to assess moral traits (such as trustworthiness, loyalty, and compassion) accurately from a limited set of observations would have provided a real advantage to our ancestors, as would the ability to keep track of people who possessed those traits over extended periods of time. These abilities would help an individual avoid cheaters, psychopaths, and murderers, and also provide the benefits that come from being surrounded by trustworthy, loyal, and cooperative individuals.

If the ability to evaluate individuals on the moral dimension provided such a tangible evolutionary benefit, we would expect to find that the tendency to make such evaluations is a basic, universal feature of human psychology. There is growing evidence that it is. A great deal of research in social psychology has demonstrated that individuals easily arrive at conclusions about the dispositions of others (and are motivated to so) with only minimal information.[16] This appears especially true for those qualities associated with moral character. For instance, within seconds of meeting a stranger people make judgments about whether she is trustworthy.[17] The tendency to make these moral evaluations appears to be common in individuals across various cultures,[18] and emerges very early in life.[19]

Moreover, individuals continue evaluating others on the moral dimension beyond this initial assessment by using a variety of methods. For instance, people infer the presence of moral traits by observing the emotional reactions and displays of others,[20] and acquire information about the presence (and absence) of moral traits by gossiping about others.[21] In short, people appear motivated to use whatever information might be relevant in order to glean information about the underlying moral traits of others.[22]

One reliable way to discover an individual's moral traits is to acquire information about that individual's reputation—to learn what is already known about a person's previous actions and whether or not he or she can be trusted. This is likely one of the basic motivations behind the fairly universal practice of gossip.[23] Researchers have shown that the ability and motivation to keep track of others' reputations predict success in economic games designed to mimic the basic features of social interaction over time.[24] In addition, research has shown that individuals display a moral memory bias—individuals are more likely to remember the faces of individuals who help them unexpectedly, and an "immoral" memory bias for those who cheat them unexpectedly in an economic game.[25] In short, the motivation to evaluate others on a moral dimension appears to be a fundamental characteristic of human social cognition, and for good reason.

The growing evidence for this moral motivation to evaluate others offers another explanation for the popularity of the supervillain, then. The fact that human beings are motivated to identify and condemn the bad guy is consistent with the fact that doing so may be a fundamentally pleasurable endeavor. This, after all, is how motivation works for behaviors in the service of many basic human needs, such as eating, sleeping, and having sex. Individuals do not engage in these behaviors out of an explicit, dispassionate calculation that these actions are required to survive and reproduce. Rather, people engage in them because they find them to be intrinsically pleasurable. Making an adaptive behavior feel good is one of the most efficient ways in which evolution serves the interests of the organism's genes. Take sex: natural selection likely favored individuals who found sex to be intrinsically pleasurable, and who were motivated to seek sexual pleasure with minimal contemplation about its reproductive consequences (although sexual selection pressures were likely different for men and women—the consequences of reproduction are more serious for women, after all—the fact that both men and women must engage in sexual intercourse in order for successful reproduction to occur likely ensured some similarities in this domain). After all, if individuals considered the pros and cons of their actions each time they engaged in sex, it is very possible that the rates of human reproduction would be far smaller.

Similarly, the pleasure individuals derive from the exercise of moral judgment—even for fictional characters—may be a result of the advantages provided by possessing the deep motivation to evaluate others morally. Supervillains, who possess a set of exaggerated moral features that make them especially easy to identify and condemn as evil, may have become popular because they push all the right moral buttons (much as individuals prefer the taste of sugary, fatty foods, because they are exaggerations of the naturally occurring cues that a food is safe and nutritious). Such moral exercises are even more likely to be pleasurable given that accurately distinguishing between good guys and bad guys with in the real world is challenging, while in the fictional worlds of superheroes and supervillains it is trivially easy.

MORAL CARICATURES

Unfortunately, the instant moral satisfaction these stories provide is not likely to be of any real help in real-world moral evaluation. The characterizations of good and evil that comic book readers find so entertaining are, in the end, gross caricatures that hopelessly distort the real nature of immorality in everyday life. Unlike in superhero comics, the presence of evil in real life is not marked by the presence of loud, unambiguous cues. Real evildoers are not especially prone to dress in black, rub their hands excessively, or twirl their mustaches. And the greatest evils in the world are likely committed as a result of the collective action or inaction of groups of individuals, often out of ignorance or even idealistic aspirations, rather than as the fulfillment of a single individual's evil plan.[26] One of the central insights gained from decades of social psychological research is that even when a single agent commits an evil deed, it is often a normal person acting under the pressure of a particular situation. This insight is nicely summarized in an unlikely source—an article outlining tips for aspiring writers. In the article, the author exhorts the would-be writer to avoid the use of caricatured villains in their writing, while offering as good a summary on the psychology of evil as has been made by any social psychologist:

> In the real world there are no villains. No one actually sets out to do evil. Yes, there are madmen and murderers and rapists and crooked politicians and greedy land developers and all sorts of villainous behaviors. But each of those people believes that he is doing what is necessary, and maybe even good… There are no villains cackling and rubbing their hands in glee as they contemplate their evil deeds. There are only people with problems, struggling to solve them.[27]

This insight represents a shift in our understanding of evil. As Baumeister[28] points out, the fact that most people who do evil do not regard themselves or their actions as evil leads to the importance for social scientists to move away from the question of evil in its classic form ("why does evil exist?"), and toward a different set of questions, such as understanding the situational forces that allow normal people to act in ways that many would consider evil.

Comic-book-style images of evildoers, in the end, make this task difficult. They may likely make people even less likely to recognize actual evildoers in their midst. After all, the real bad guys never resemble the images from the Batman movies.

CONCLUSION: MORAL PORNOGRAPHY

We have used this chapter and its discussion of comic books to articulate a quietly radical idea. The history of moral psychology has focused relentlessly on judgments of particular actions, from the widely used vignette about whether it is right for Heinz to steal the medicine to save his wife's life, to the recent fascination with the problem of whether it is right to change the course of a runaway trolley so as to save five lives, even if that means that one (different) person will be killed.[29]

Against that heavy focus on actions, we suggest that moral judgment is about judging *people*. Establishing the moral character of particular individuals is a vitally important feature of everyday life and can have immense practical significance, one that potentially affects our survival. Deciding whether someone's action was morally right or wrong is itself of little importance, insofar as the act lies in the past and cannot be changed. But knowing the moral character of a person is useful for predicting that person's future behavior, which carries a host of implications regarding how to act vis-à-vis that person from now on.

Indeed, if there is any innate predisposition to make moral judgments, then its evolutionary basis must have been by facilitating survival and reproduction—for which predicting the future of interaction partners is far more relevant than passing judgment on their past actions. Hence as theorists have begun to consider evolutionary bases for moral judgment, we think they will have to begin to focus more on judging people than judging actions.

Judging people and predicting their future actions is hard. The most violent criminals are violent in only a tiny fraction of their behaviors. (Indeed, the highest frequencies of physical violence are still limited to about 25 percent of interactions—and these rates are found only among 2-year-old children![30]). So-called liars tell the truth most of the time. Hence, perhaps, the hugely skewed bias in moral judgment, which boldly makes strong inferences about moral character and predictions about future behavior based on only a small number of immoral actions. Yet of course such prediction is tricky. Someone who lied may be labeled a "liar" but may only lie in certain contexts, or even lie once and tell the truth from then on.

It is no wonder, then, that the supervillain fascinates. Magneto and his so-called Brotherhood of Evil Mutants present no morally ambiguous cases for the nonmutant population—humans know exactly what to expect. They do bad things (and enjoy them) routinely. Their past actions are a reliable guide to their future actions.

We have described comic books as moral pornography. The term "pornography" is, of course, borrowed from the domain of sexuality. One interesting feature is the striking gender differences in the rates in which pornography is consumed. In one recent study, for instance, a little fewer than 14 percent of women (in a sample of young adults aged 18–30) reported that they had viewed pornography in the past week. For men, that number was 63 percent.[31] This may come as no surprise—most young men want more sex than they get, thanks in part to the greater male than female desire for sex.[32] Many invest considerable time, energy, and money in courting a desired woman, despite a high likelihood that she will end up refusing his sexual advances. But there is no alternative:

they cannot know in advance whether their investment will lead to sex. The world depicted in pornography, in which the female characters are typically willing and often eager to have sex—usually without requiring the male characters to invest much time, energy, or money—thus offers great appeal to men. It is, after all, a world where strong desire is fulfilled and effort is not necessary.

Likewise, we have suggested that the real world is one in which bad is stronger than good. When the two clash on equal grounds, bad tends to win because of its greater power (and can be defeated only when greatly outnumbered). But the satisfaction of superhero comics comes from their depiction of a universe in which good is stronger than bad: a universe in which superheroes—even when outnumbered—win almost every time. Just as sexual pornography depicts a world where the desired outcomes occur reliably and the difficulties and ambiguities of actual life are pleasantly and effortlessly absent, comic books depict a world where desired outcomes occur reliably (good triumphs over evil) and the difficulties and ambiguities of moral prediction are absent.

NOTES

1. Ferry, D. (1993). *Gilgamesh: A new rendering in English verse*. New York: Farrar, Straus and Giroux.
2. Haidt, J., Rosenberg, E., & Hom, H. (2003). Differentiating diversities: Moral diversity is not like other kinds. *Journal of Applied Social Psychology*, *33*, 1–36.
3. Top 100 Comic Book Villains of All Time. (2009). Retrieved July 17, 2011, from http://comics.ign.com/top-100-villains/index.html.
4. All Time World Box Office Grosses. (2011). Retrieved July 17, 2011, from http://boxofficemojo.com/alltime/world/
5. Shawcross, J. T. (1998). An early view of Satan as hero of *Paradise Lost*. *Milton Quarterly*, *32*, 104–105.

6. Baumeister, R. F., Bratslavsky, E., Finkenauer, C., & Vohs, K. D. (2001). Bad is stronger than good. *Review of General Psychology, 5,* 323–370.
7. Gray, K. (2010). Moral transformation: Good and evil turn the weak into the mighty. *Social Psychological and Personality Science, 1,* 253–258.
8. For a discussion, see Baumeister, Bratslavsky, et al. (2001).
9. Baumeister, R. F., Catanese, K. R., & Vohs, K. D. (2001). Is there a gender difference in strength of sex drive? Theoretical views, conceptual distinctions, and a review of relevant evidence. *Personality and Social Psychology Review, 5,* 242–273.
10. Senn, B. (1996). *Golden horrors: An illustrated critical filmography of terror cinema, 1931–1939.* Jefferson, NC: McFarland.
11. Trilling, L. (1971). *Sincerity and authenticity.* Cambridge, MA: Harvard.
12. Axelrod, R., & Hamilton, W. D. (1981). The evolution of cooperation. *Science, 211,* 1390–1396.
    Trivers, R. L. (1971). The evolution of reciprocal altruism. *Quarterly Review of Biology, 46,* 35–57.
13. Frank, R. H. (1988). *Passions within reason: The strategic role of the emotions.* New York: Norton.
14. Sanfey, A. G., Rilling, J. K., Aronson, J. A., Nystrom, L. E., & Cohen, J. D. (2003). The neural basis of economic decision-making in the ultimatum game. *Science, 300,* 1755–1758.
    Tabibnia, G., Satpute, A. B., & Lieberman, M. D. (2008). The sunny side of fairness: Preference for fairness activates reward circuitry (and disregarding fairness activates self-control circuitry. *Psychological Science, 19,* 339–347.
15. Gintis, H., Henrich, J., Bowles, S., Boyd, R., & Fehr, E. (2008). Strong reciprocity and the roots of human morality. *Social Justice Research, 21,* 241–253.

16. Gilbert, D. T. (1998). Ordinary personology. In D. T. Gilbert, S. T. Fiske, & G. Lindzey (Eds.), *The handbook of social psychology (4th edition)*. New York: McGraw Hill.
    Gilbert, D. T., & Malone, P. S. (1995). The correspondence bias. *Psychological Bulletin*, *117*, 21–38.
17. Bar, M., Neta, M., & Linz, H. (2006). Very first impressions. *Emotion*, *6*, 269–278.
    Todorov, A., Said, C. P., Engell, A. D., & Oosterhof, N. N. (2008). Understanding evaluation of faces on social dimensions. *Trends in Cognitive Sciences*, *12*, 455–460.
18. Fiske, S. T., Cuddy, A. J. C., & Glick, P. (2007). First judge warmth, then competence: Fundamental social dimensions. *Trends in Cognitive Sciences*, *11*, 77–83.
19. Hamlin, J. K., Wynn, K., & Bloom, P. (2007). Social evaluation by preverbal infants. *Nature*, *450*, 557–559.
    Kuhlmeier, V., Wynn, K., & Bloom, P. (2003). Attribution of dispositional states by 12-month-olds. *Psychological Science*, *14*, 402–408.
20. Ames, D. R., & Johar, G. V. (2009). I'll know what you're like when I see how you feel. *Psychological Science*, *20*, 586–593. See also Frank (1988).
21. Foster, E. K. (2004). Research on gossip: Taxonomy, methods, and future directions. *Review of General Psychology*, *8*, 78–99.
22. Pizarro, D. A. & Tannenbaum, D. (2012). Bringing character back: How the motivation to evaluate character influences judgments of moral blame. In M. Mikulincer & P. Shaver, (Eds.), *The social psychology of morality: Exploring the causes of good and evil.* Washington, DC: American Psychological Association.
23. See, e.g., Baumeister, R. F., Zhang, L., & Vohs, K. D. (2004). Gossip as cultural learning. *Review of General Psychology*, *8*, 111–121.
24. See, e.g., Rand D. G., Dreber A., Ellingsen, T., Fudenberg, D., & Nowak M. A. (2009). Positive interactions promote public cooperation. *Science*, *325*, 1272–1275.

25. Chang, L. J., & Sanfey, A.G. (2009). Unforgettable ultimatums? Expectation violations promote enhanced social memory following economic exchange. *Frontiers in Behavioral Neuroscience*, *3*, 1–12.
26. See, e.g., Baumeister, R. F. (1997). *Evil: Inside human violence and cruelty*. New York: Freeman.
27. Bova, B. (n.d.). Tips for writers. Retrieved from http://benbova.com/tips2.html.
28. Baumeister(1997).
29. Pizarro & Tannenbaum (2012).
30. See Tremblay, R. E. (2000). The development of aggressive behavior during childhood: What have we learned in the past century? *International Journal of Behavioral Development*, *24*, 129–141.
    Tremblay, R. E. (2003). Why socialization fails: The case of chronic physical aggression. In B. B. Lahey, T. E. Moffitt, & A. Caspi (Eds.), *The causes of conduct disorder and serious juvenile delinquency* (pp. 182–224). New York: Guilford Press.
    Tremblay, R. E., Nagin, D. S., Sguin, J. R., Zoccolillo, M., Zelazo, P. D. Boivin, M., Prusse, D., & Japel, C. (2004). Physical aggression during early childhood: Trajectories and predictors. *Pediatrics*, *114*, e43–e50.
31. Hald, G.H. (2006). Gender differences in pornography consumption among young heterosexual Danish adults. *Archives of Sexual Behavior*, *35*, 577–585.
32. Baumeister, Catanese, & Vohs (2001).

THREE

Are Superhero Stories Good for Us?

Reflections from Clinical Practice

Lawrence C. Rubin

EDITOR'S NOTE

Superheroes and their stories can affect us—as children and as adults—in positive, even transformative ways. Larry Rubin explores exactly this question as he uses his clinical and research experience to discuss the different ways that superheroes' stories touch us.

—Robin S. Rosenberg

Carmen was 5 years old when her parents brought her and her siblings to New York from Puerto Rico. She and her brother Julio loved their trips to the local candy store where they bought comic books—he favored Captain America, and she was a Superman fan. They enjoyed reading their treasured stories to each other, but even more so to their mother, whose English skills improved with each shared adventure. Even as Carmen grew to adulthood, her appreciation for and fond memories of the role that superhero stories played in her family lived strongly within her. It was for this reason that when her second child Roberto reached the age of appreciation, that she would read Superman comics to him in hopes of helping him to read, but more importantly, to understand better the adventure that had given him a forever family. For just as the infant Kal-El had traveled from the planet Krypton and the loving arms of his parents Jor-El and Lara, so too had Roberto come a long distance—from an orphanage in Honduras. While comic book adventures ultimately lessened his anxiety around reading, Roberto's mother was, in essence building his vocabulary around the narrative of adoption. With each Superman tale, and ensuing discussion about adoption, Roberto better understood that his life was a story unfolding. His Kryptonian counterpart had traveled light years through space to find just the right family. He too had traversed a great distance to the welcoming arms of his adoptive family. And just as Kal-El had to reconcile loss with connection, so too did Robert have to make sense of how he could, at the same time, be loved and "given away." For both Roberto and Kal-El, great pain had to be endured, many questions had to be asked and answered, a sense of identity forged, and deep soul searching had to be done. When I met Roberto, he was on his adventure, talking to people and sharing his adoption narrative and the lessons that comics, particularly Superman taught him. To this day, Roberto loves all things superheroic, wears the emblem of Superman about his neck, has a deep and abiding respect for adoption, and a profound love for the family that opened its heart to him.

I met Roberto, or should I say, Roberto found me shortly after the release of my book, *Using Superheroes in Counseling and Play Therapy* (2006). He was a dyed-in the wool, card-carrying superhero fan, with a deep and abiding love for all things Superman, and a childlike passion that I admired. He wore a magnificent hand-crafted metal pendant around his neck (a cousin to the Superman tattoo that I concealed beneath my shirt). Looking back, however, it was not Roberto's love for Superman that intrigued me as much as it was the role that the superhero played in the unfolding adoption narrative of his life. As an adoptive parent, a former child who loved (and still loves) Superman, and a therapist who uses superheroes in my clinical work, I appreciate, more than anything else, the story that Roberto (and later, his mother) shared with me. So, when I was asked to choose a topic for an essay in this volume, the choice seemed to pick me. I would talk about superhero stories, and why I believe they can be good for us. And rather than argue from an empirical and statistical perspective, I will reflect on voices that along with my own have found value in the story of the superhero, in the telling of superhero stories.

My contention in this essay is that the superhero mythos is a rich, complex and multilayered metaphor that appeals to readers and enthusiasts of all ages, and that carries with it the seeds for self-understanding, problem resolution, identity formation, resiliency, and growth. If we can move beyond the narrow typecasting of the superhero as hyperaggressive vigilante (which some indeed are), the comic book as a marginalized and diminutive literary form, and the superhero movie as just another avenue for Hollywood exploitation, then we free superheroes to reveal their secret identities—as mirrors into ourselves and vehicles for insight into all facets of the human condition.

FANTASY STORIES—REAL LIVES

Since they leapt from comic book pages in the late 1930s, superheroes have captured our imaginations. They have flown, moved mountains, traveled through time, and changed the course of history, all while trying to lead otherwise normal lives. Their origin stories have been similarly intriguing. Hurtled to Earth from distant galaxies, born of genetic mutation or transformed through scientific experiment gone awry, these colorful characters have struggled to fit in. While early superheroes were "black and white figures with a very simplistic goal-protecting the world from evil,"[1] the world and its evil have become more complex over the decades. And in turn, superheroes and their stories have become more involved in addressing "real-world" situations including poverty, racism, homophobia, global warming, and terrorism scenarios.

The physically and often psychologically flawless superheroes of the "golden age" of comics (1930s to 1950s), gave way to their deeply flawed "silver age" (1960s to 1990s) successors through a process that comic historians Lang and Trimble called "progressive demythification."[2] Through this evolution, superheroes have lost their "otherworldliness" and sensationalistic aura and have become more human. Flaws become every bit as important in the superhero tale as do strengths; moral certainty gives way to moral ambiguity as superheroes battle demons, both internal and external. As former Marvel group editor Danny Fingeroth suggested in his treatise on superheroes, the silver age incorporated a larger vocabulary, more complicated plots, and an attempt at character development.[3]

It is within this "real world" of human experience that the stories of flawed superheroes have gained and maintained their appeal, up through the modern era of comics. The comic book world is no longer one of fantasy and fiction, but one that more and more closely resembles reality. While their secret identities are constantly threatened, their powers the target of villainous plots, and their loved ones always at risk for imminent harm, superheroes do ultimately prevail. However it comes at the cost of constant inner torment, alienation, and uncertainty. Quoting fictional superhero Billy Button, aka Captain Mantra, Paul Gravett in *Superheroes: Nothing Will Ever Be the Same Again* notes that "it's not a comic book world anymore.... Our time has passed. Problems don't come in neat little boxes anymore, with 'The End' scrawled in the corner. There is no end. Only new versions of reality. People don't talk in balloons anymore. They curse. They shout obscenities. The world is no place for children or heroes which may be the same thing."[4]

Is this trend due to the increasing complexity of modern society, the growing sophistication (and age) of the average comic book reader and superhero moviegoer? Is it born of our desire to create these characters in our own (flawed) image? Or is it that we simply need to close the distance between ourselves and these formally "perfect" characters in order to create a means of better expressing our own existential dilemmas...and then develop means for surmounting them? Whatever the reason, our collective need for more "realistic" heroes has resulted in a powerful trend in comic book literature to feature stories that everyday "nonsuperheroes" can identify with. Startling images and powerful stories abound of superheroes struggling to understand and help. These include Spider-Man at the ruins of the World Trade Center; Tony Stark, aka Iron Man, staring down his alcoholic reflection in a mirror; Ben Grimm, aka The Thing, returning to the anti-Semitic streets of his childhood; Speedy, Green Arrow's sidekick, wrestling with her HIV diagnosis; and the Incredible Hulk proclaiming war against those who betrayed him. There have even been numerous comic book and graphic novels featuring stories of superheroes, including Bruce Banner, Peter Parker, and Robert Reynolds, aka the Sentry, undergoing their own counseling and psychotherapy.[5] These are as much human dramas as they are fantastic tales. And it is these stories of fantastic individuals wrestling with everyday issues and challenges that are so compelling.

A CRY FOR MYTH

Humans are meaning-makers! By virtue of our capacity to reflect both inwardly and outwardly, to move forward and backward through time, and to imagine possibilities, we have the unique ability to weave together the threads of our existence into meaning and narratives. Our history on the planet is marked by stories, from the creation myths of ancient, long-gone civilizations to the contemporary narratives that populate our literature, cinema, and "real-world" stage.

Myths and legends are a reflection of our lived experience, captured in word and image. They are humanity's attempts to answer these fundamental questions: "Who are we?" "How did we get here?" "What is the meaning of the journey?" and "How do we overcome obstacles?" American writer Joseph Campbell believed that myths serve numerous vital functions such as offering a model of the universe, validating the social order, providing guidance through life and most importantly, maintaining "awe."[6] Even more important for Campbell, myths provide clues to being alive. Along similar lines, cultural critic Richard Slotkin suggested that myths dramatize personal and cultural narratives, recapitulate history, are prescriptions for action, and reduce incalculable centuries of human experience to understandable metaphor.[7]

In answering the question of what effect superhero stories have on us, it is important to place these tales into historical perspective, and to see them in a spectrum that includes other world mythologies. In their *Myth of the American Superhero*, John Lawrence and Robert Jewett suggested that the tale of the superhero is no less than modern-day mythology, which, in spite of its many forms and characters, has effects arguably as profound and important as its literary ancestors.[8] This position is contrary to that of psychologist Rollo May, who in *The Cry for Myth*, announced that contemporary societies have lost their direction because their mythologies, and by association, their histories have been marginalized, if not completely eradicated.[9]

Lawrence and Jewett believed that it was the superhero story, or "American monomyth," with its historical epicenter in the American Revolution and later in the conquest of the Wild West, that seemed to revitalize what they considered our society's eroded historical and moral foundation. The myth of the American superhero, which centered on the selfless hero's redemptive mission to restore a threatened community to its formerly paradisiacal state, while illusory, was important in forming the mythos of the American spirit. In this context, it becomes easy to see why superhero stories are so powerful. Just like their mythological forerunners, they offer hope, provide a stage on which deeply human passion plays can be enacted, and most importantly, and once again, offer us heroes to inspire, guide, and teach. Whether it is Superman attempting (and later apologizing for his inability) to rid the world of nuclear weapons, the Fantastic Four sacrificing themselves to save the planet from deadly cosmic radiation, the Watchmen bringing order to a misguided society, the aging Spider-Man reminding us of the dignity of our later years, or the Powerpuff Girls reminding us of our inherent strengths and potentialities, these stories inspire us to transcend personal and perhaps even societal limits, to test out our moral wings, and to flex our cognitive, interpersonal, and emotional muscles.

WRITING OUR OWN PERSONAL MYTHOLOGY

Stories of superheroes, those larger-than-life figures, can inspire us by providing metaphors for overcoming obstacles, defeating enemies—both internal and external, and mastering seemingly insurmountable challenges. These near-mythic tales can indeed exert a powerful influence in our lives, but not as much, perhaps, as the stories that we build about ourselves. The notion that life and its often painful trials can be conceptualized as an unfolding narrative story is powerfully anchored in the related psychological fields of narrative identity research[10] and narrative therapy.[11] According to Michael White,[12] storytelling, as an unfolding linear process, helps us to recognize, monitor, and effect change over time. White describes "coherent sequences," referring to the use of narrative, and suggests that we each have the ability to construct our life stories in a way that is potentially fulfilling. By doing so, past and present, successes and failures, heroes and villains can be anchored in a cohesive story that helps us to make sense of the seemingly disparate and disconnected experiences and relationships in our lives. Tilmann Habermas and his intellectual colleagues, including Kate McLean,[13] have studied the manner in which people build coherent autobiographies, and determined that the life stories that best serve us are those that have temporal, causal, and thematic elements. Similarly, Pennebaker and Seagal[14] researched the potential health benefits of narrative, and determined that writing or telling one's story helps the individual in a number of ways, including mastery through simplification, control through catharsis, and mastery through expression. For these researchers, it is even possible to work through and resolve trauma by organizing the traumatic events and feelings into a coherent and life-affirming narrative.

Linking this realm of narrative identity research to the concept of "personal mythology" is the work of David Feinstein[15] and Jefferson Singer,[16] who believed that just as cultural symbols and archetypes are housed in a collective unconscious, our memories, perceptions, dreams, and behaviors are stored in mythic fields within each of us. For Feinstein, the stories of superheroes are so deeply resonant because their elements and characters are, in an unspoken way, familiar to us. For Singer, these stories can provide a lens through which we can filter important life experiences that have the power to "raise our spirits, guide our actions and influence others."[17] According to these researchers, we automatically understand Clark Kent and Bruce Wayne's pain of parental loss, Peter Parker's adolescent angst, the Hulk's and Thing's deep sense of alienation and shame, as well as Wolverine and Elektra's deep-seated anger. Similarly, we can rejoice along with each of our hero's conquests, romantic victories, and successes over adversity. Superhero stories help us to integrate elements of our own narrative adventures by providing a link to others, as well as missing links in the chain of events in our lives.

SUPERHEROES TO THE RESCUE

If superhero stories provide a much-needed modern day equivalent to tales of mythological heroes, can they also provide a similarly useful function for the individual? If, as James Hillman suggested, mythology was the psychology of antiquity and psychology is the mythology of modernity,[18] can we then mine superhero stories for wisdom that can actually help the individual?

Clients come to counseling in order to share their stories of sadness, failure, inadequacy, and loss, and as such, are often tellers of tragic tales. Counseling can provide clients with the opportunity to rewrite their stories, placing the counselor in the role of myth-maker. Seen as such, the counselors can assist their client to integrate past, present, and future events, while building cohesive, useful, and nonpathological stories that affirm strength, success, and resilience.[19] If clients can learn to reframe their lives as unfolding personal mythologies, rather than as finite and finished stories, then they have the opportunity to reemerge from the adversities of their lives as heroes in their own minds rather than failures. In this regard, it has been suggested that the creation and use of narrative in therapy to overcome adversity is potentially healing, in that it allows clients to assimilate problematic experiences into their schemas, and indirectly express painful experiences.[20] And this is where superheroes come into the picture.

Scores of children, teens, and adults spend countless hours following the exploits of superheroes—those larger-than-life characters that can do things they can only imagine. It has been estimated that each year, hundreds of millions of superhero comics are bought, sold, and traded[21] and that superhero movies (*Spider-Man*,

Batman, and *Transformers*), and mythological heroic adventures (*Star Wars*, *Lord of the Rings*, and *Harry Potter*) are wildly popular at the box office. Their sheer volume in sales, whether tied to marketing, big-action movie budgeting, or even the banal need for the next big slam-bang-crash story indicates that superhero movies are an important part of our media landscape and consciousness.

If people in therapy are potential heroes in their own evolving mythologies, then therapists are somewhere between guardians and mentors. If we think of these mythologies in terms of superhero stories, then therapists may be conceptualized as sidekicks. In many superhero tales, it is the sidekick that sees the larger picture; in contrast, the hero's vision is focused on the enemy or task at hand. It is the sidekick, who, unencumbered by ego, is able to perform without the burden of pride, while the hero falters and falls. The sidekick is available to remind us about the limits of absolute power, as he (or she) is often weak and without unique (super) power. Without the sidekick, the hero is often alone in the fight against his or her demons, and without the calm, collected, and contextual wisdom or even humor that the sidekick often manifests. The sidekick is, in this way, a socializing agent for the hero, who is often accustomed to charging into the fray- impulses, powers, and weapons drawn. And finally, the sidekick is, in a therapeutic sense, a reflective audience or reflecting team for the hero, ever ready to share his opinions, insights, and wisdom. I have had the privilege of being the sidekick to many clients, young and old; sharing their journeys and hearing their stories. In these instances, their stories were most definitely utilized in the service of self-awareness, growth, and healing. A few short examples will illustrate.

A 5-year-old girl spent numerous sessions on the floor of my clinical playroom, carefully assigning superhero action figures to either the "bad side" or "good side." The violence and destructiveness in her weekly superhero battles mirrored the painful and often aggressive battles between her warring parents. As tensions between the parents ebbed and flowed, so too did the violence in the superhero play. When finally the parents reconciled, the child's play began to contain themes of helping and healing. The savagery in her battles gave way to détente and friendship.

Another example is that of an 8-year-old boy with a long diagnostic pedigree (attention-deficit/hyperactivity disorder, obsessive-compulsive disorder, conduct disorder), who played out deeply painful feelings of personal inadequacy and loneliness through his alter-ego, a fire-breathing dragon hand puppet, which he aptly named "psycho-monster." Intuitively, he understood that he was different from the other children, and that adults looked on him with a combination of annoyance, confusion, and disdain. I believe that he also recognized that children kept their distance from him and as a result, he poignantly felt the sting of ostracism and rejection. In his play-battles, "psycho-monster" was often vanquished by the other characters, most often superheroes. They ganged up against him, with the exception of Wonder Woman. It was this kind, powerful, confident and nurturing mother-figure that would invariably come to the rescue of the besieged puppet, wrestling him back from the brink of destruction and into the warm loving arms of safety and acceptance.

A final example: During a workshop presentation on the role of superheroes in psychotherapy and counseling, a middle-aged female therapist fondly recalled the many hours she spent as a child in the 1940s and 1950s following the exploits of Wonder Woman. She was particularly enthralled by her heroine's ability to balance being "just a regular person" with the demands of superheroism. She found Wonder Woman's strength, intelligence, guilelessness, and ability to stand up to men amazing qualities that she wanted to emulate, both during childhood and into adulthood. Later in life, as a therapist, she often drew on memories of Wonder Woman and her own internalized superheroic qualities when working with challenging clients as well as when trying to cope with the many challenges in her own life, most notably loss. Just as truth was important to her heroine, so too was truthfulness an important theme in her adult relationship and therapeutic work with women who had suffered trauma and loss during their childhoods and teen years. Each of these people was able to draw on and meaningfully integrate the messages within superhero stories into their own lives.

MORAL LESSONS LEARNED

Superheroes are magnificent inventions. They are capable of the most amazing feats of will and strength. While each is different in his or her own way, all superheroes share a core set of characteristics, one of which is unflagging dedication to uphold justice and to act as moral beacons.[22] While most of us don't actually believe that we can fly, travel through time, or bend steel in our bare hands, it is through imagination and our vicarious adventures alongside of superheroes, that we can explore the world of possibilities, both outer and inner. These stories allow us to harness the power of imagination, that fertile field of possibility that lies within each of us. One of the most interesting roles that superhero stories play is in stimulating what psychologist Michael Pardales calls "moral imagination."[23] For him, moral imagination is a playground of sorts, on which we experiment with our potential and rework our personal rendering of the line that separates right from wrong. By standing (or flying, as the case may be) alongside Spider-Man as he perennially wrestles with his conscience, with Elektra as she chooses between being the strongest warrior or the best student, with Wolverine as he struggles to relinquish his angry and solitary ways in favor of being a team-member, with Magneto and Professor Xavier as they clash for supremacy in an morally diffuse world, or with the Silver

Surfer as he must decide to renounce his tie to Galactus in order to save Earth,[24] we are given the opportunity to stretch our own moral imaginations by wondering along with these heroes about the most appropriate and correct course of action. We must, along with these characters, choose between right and wrong, strength and vulnerability, power and humility, vigilantism and cooperation, as well as between isolation and teamplay.

In an effort to draw practical significance from Pardales's work, Justin Martin queried fourth graders regarding their knowledge of important superhero attributes, and then correlated those with their own self-perceptions.[25] He found that, in general, children who valued morality in their favorite superheroes also placed a high value on being moral people in their own lives. They seemed drawn to particular superheroes, not because of those heroes' strength and powers per se, but because they appreciated the moral passion plays and the superhero's ability to maintain a moral stance. In doing so, Martin demonstrated that the moral conflicts and messages in superhero stories actually resonate with and inform children's moral attitudes, shaping, in a very real-world way, the manner in which they evaluate themselves and the behavior of others. While children don't fight crime, except in their imaginations, and adults don't usually have to make life-or-death decisions, especially on a grand scale, superhero stories represent moral metaphors that the rest of us can apply to our everyday lives. The very slogans of the most popular superheroes suggest that they are ready-made moral educators. Superman battles for "truth, justice and the American way," and Spider-Man must continually draw on his Uncle Ben's axiom, "with great power, there must also come great responsibility." Superheroes must continually decide between personal gain and the greater good and whether to avenge victims through violent means or to bring their enemies to justice. Peter DeScioli suggests that superhero myths provide us with the opportunity to experiment with questions of morality.[26]

CONCLUSION

I have personally witnessed the transformative power of superhero stories in my own evolving personal narrative and in my therapeutic work. Each element of the superhero myth provides endless possibilities for restorying. The origin stories of many superheroes contain poignant elements of parental abuse, loss, and death, such as young Bruce Wayne's witnessing of his parents' murder and Bruce Banner's genetic exploitation by his megalomaniacal father. The constant pressure on superheroes to maintain their secret identities inevitably positions them as angst-ridden outsiders, forever trying to feel whole, as in Peter Parker's endless quest to be like every other teenager. And then there are those magnificent superpowers, sometimes known to the superhero, while at other times only hinted at as they awkwardly fumble their way into adulthood and maturity, such as young Clark Kent's eventual awakening to his full potential. Finally, there is the villain; that demonic, and often equally powerful nemesis who continually compels the superhero to look deeply into and question the very basis for their own humanity. The Joker is always reminding Batman just how alike they are!

Each of these superheroes, and countless others in their illustrious pantheon, have provided generations of moviegoers and comic book readers with stories and the opportunity to ask and answer important questions in their own lives.

NOTES

1a. Rubin, L. (Ed.) (2006). *Using superheroes in counseling and play therapy*. New York: Springer.

1. Hughes, J (2006). Who watches the Watchmen?: Ideology and "real world" superheroes. *Journal of Popular Culture, 39*(4), 546–557. Quote on p. 546.

2. Lang, J., & Trimble, P. (1988). Whatever happened to the man of tomorrow?: An examination of the American monomyth and the comic book superhero. *Journal of Popular Culture*, *22*(3), 157–173.
3. Fingeroth, D. (2004). *Superman on the couch: What superheroes really tell us about ourselves and our society*. New York: Continuum.
4. Gravett, P. (2007). *Superheroes: Nothing will ever be the same again*. Retrieved May 20, 2010 from http://www.paulgravett.com/index.php/articles/article/superheroes.
5. Rubin, L. (2012). Superheroes on the couch: Exploring our limits. *Journal of Popular Culture, 45,* 410–431.
6. Campbell, J. (1956). *The hero with a thousand faces*. New York: Meridian Press.Campbell, J. (1972). *Myths to live by*. New York: Bantam.
7. Slotkin, R. (2000). *Regeneration through violence: The mythology of the American frontier (1600–1860)*. Norman: University of Oklahoma Press.
8. Lawrence, J. S., & Jewett, R. (2002). *The myth of the American superhero*. London Eerdmans.
9. May, R. (1991). *The cry for myth*. New York: Delta.
10. Habermas, T. (2007). How to tell a life. *Journal of Cognition and Development, 8*(1), 1–31.
    Habermas, T., & de Silveira, C. (2008). The development of global coherence in life narratives across adolescence: Temporal, causal, and thematic elements. *Developmental Psychology*, *44*(3), 707–721.
    McLean, K. (2008). Stories of the young and old: Personal continuity and narrative identity. *Developmental Psychology*, *44*(1), 254–264.
    Pennebaker, J., & Seagal, J. (1999). Forming a story: The health benefits of narrative. *Journal of Clinical Psychology*, *55*(10), 1243–1254.
    Singer, J. (2004). Narrative identity and meaning making across the adult lifespan: An introduction. *Journal of Personality*, *72*, 437–460.
11. White, M., & Epston, D. (1990). *Narrative means to therapeutic ends*. New York: Norton.
12. White & Epston (1990).
13. Habermas (2007); McLean (2008).
14. Pennebaker & Seagal (1999)

15. Feinstein, D. (1998). Personal mythology and psychotherapy: Mythmaking in psychological and spiritual development. *American Journal of Orthopsychiatry*, *67*, 508–521.
16. Singer (2004).
17. Singer (2004), p. 442.
18. Hillman, J. (1979). *The dream and the underworld.* New York: Harper & Row.
19. Lukoff, D. (1997). The psychologist as mythologist. *The Journal of Humanistic Psychology*, *37*(3), 34–68.
20. Hermans, H. (1999). Self-narrative as meaning construction: The dynamics of self-investigation. *Journal of Clinical Psychology*, *55*(10), 1193–1211.

    Stiles, W., Honos-Webb, L., & Lani, J. (1999). Some functions of narrative in the assimilation of problematic experiences. *Journal of Clinical Psychology*, *55*(10), 1213–1226.
21. Stewart, S., & Kahan, J. (2006). *Caped Crusaders 101: Composition through comic books*. Jefferson, NC: McFarland.
22. Reynolds, R. (1992). *Super heroes: A modern mythology*. Jackson: University of Mississippi Press.
23. Pardales, M. J. (2002). So, how did you arrive at that decision?: Connecting moral imagination and moral judgment. *Journal of Moral Education*, *31*(4), 429–436.
24. Gabilliet, J. (1994). Cultural and mythical aspects of a superhero: The Silver Surfer, 1968–1970. *Journal of Popular Culture*, *28*(2), 203–213.
25. Martin, J. (2007). Children's attitudes toward superheroes as a potential indicator of moral understanding. *Journal of Moral Education*, *36*(2), 239–250.
26. DeScioli, P. (2008). Cracking the superhero's moral code. In R. Rosenberg (Ed.), *The psychology of superheroes: An unauthorized exploration* (pp. 245–259). Dallas, TX: BenBella Books.

FOUR

Emotions in Comics

Why the Silver Age of Comics Made a Difference

Peter J. Jordan

EDITOR'S NOTE

Peter Jordan's area of psychological research is emotions: emotions in organizations and emotions at work. He's in a unique position to explore how superheroes' emotions are part of what grab us. In this essay, Jordan discusses a brief history of superheroes in comics, the evolving role of emotions in their stories, and the different ways that DC and Marvel handled emotions, including conflicting emotions, and emotions of shame and pride.

—Robin S. Rosenberg

The silver age of comics was a period of reinvention of superheroes that extended from the mid 1950s to the early 1970s.[1] DC Comics was at the forefront of this silver age with revitalized characters like the Flash,[2] Green Lantern,[3] and The Atom.[4] Smith[5] notes that in the early 1960s, the Marvel publisher Martin Goodman asked Stan Lee to create a stable of superheroes to compete with DC Comics. What Stan Lee came up with was a stable of superheroes that changed the face of the paradigm. Lee started with the Fantastic Four[6] and followed with a succession of characters such as Spider-Man (introduced in *Amazing Fantasy*),[7] the X-Men,[8] and the Avengers.[9] The characters introduced by Stan Lee had something different about them that made readers connect with them immediately. In this chapter, I argue that it was the introduction of the human element, emotion, that made these superheroes so understandable and allowed readers to connect with them based on their own experience of emotions in their daily lives. I will also argue that the creation of these stories was so successful because it modeled established psychological theories in relation to emotion[10] and the link between personality and human behavior.[11]

MY EXPERIENCE OF COMICS IN THE SILVER AGE

I learned how to read through comics. As a child of the 1960s in Australia, I was taught to read by rote learning through Dick and Jane readers. My real education came from comics. In those days you were not spoiled for the choice that abounds today—you had four basic categories to choose from: War Comics (e.g., Commando), Disney comics (e.g., Goofy), adolescent comics (e.g., Archie), or superhero comics (DC and Marvel). Superhero comics were my choice, and I was lucky that I started reading during the silver age revival. In particular, living in Australia, I had easy access to DC comics so I read Green Lantern and Superman and Flash and Justice Society of America (JSA) and the Justice League of America (JLA). I loved them, and they provided a great escape. But all this changed one day when a good friend, Malcolm Barry, came to me with a Marvel comic. I was hooked. I quickly gathered a collection of Spider-Man, Daredevil, X-Men, Fantastic Four, and Avengers with occasional forays into Captain America and the Iron Man. On reflection, the first thing that attracted me to Marvel was the artwork, which seemed to me to be edgier, and the colors, which to me seemed more vibrant. But what maintained my interest was that these stories seemed to be about real people that experienced a range of emotions. The stories were not just about their powers, but about their experience of those powers and the decisions they agonized over on a day-to-day basis. What I have learned later in life is that these stories were so successful because they reflected solid psychological theory. Indeed, more than just reflecting existing psychological theories, they sometimes mirrored psychological theories that were to be articulated around the same time, and in some cases were in advance of theories that emerged much later.

THE EXPERIENCE OF EMOTIONS

Around the time Stan Lee was writing about the Fantastic Four and Spider-Man, two psychologists, Stanley Schachter and Jerome Singer, developed what was to be named the two-factor theory of emotion.[12] Simply put, this theory argues that human emotion is composed of two factors, physiological arousal and a thought process or *cognition* about that arousal. While there were plenty of trigger events for physiological arousal in DC Comics, it was Marvel that extended the story lines from physiological arousal to highlight the cognitive processes that led to the range of emotions experienced and expressed by their superheroes.

The second psychological concept to distinguish DC Comics from Marvel emerges from Psychology 101 and is the distinction of "between-person" variation and "within-person" variation.[13] Between-person variation is based on the fact that we all act differently. We have different personalities and different attitudes and different motivations, which in combination results in behavior differing between people. While between-person variation allows for some changes in behavior, there is an in-built assumption that an individual's behavior is relatively stable across different situations. This was DC comics in the 1960s. Superman was always virtuous, Batman was always serious,[14] and Green Lantern was strong-willed and without fear.[15] It did not matter what situation these characters encountered, their behavior was always consistent with the personality that their writers had developed. The major variation within the stories in this framework was confronting physical challenges and action to resolve those challenges, and the action in DC Comics was good.

Within-person variation, on the other hand, acknowledges that each of us has a set of dominant dispositions (personality, attitudes, and motivations), but accepts that our behavior can vary on a minute-to-minute basis. Unlike Superman and Batman, we are not always predictable. While the concept of within-person variation was around for a long time, this theory emerged with a firm psychological foundation when Walter Mischel and Yoshi Shoda proposed the Cognitive Affective Personality System (CAPS).[16] According to CAPS, behavior is determined by both psychological processes and by the situation the individual is experiencing. In essence, even though you may have a single dominant emotional display there are allowances for changes in this dominant disposition on a momentary basis. Let's apply this to the Hulk: he may have a single dominant display (anger), but this display is not etched into stone, and he has momentary changes in his emotional display, such as interest or curiosity when he interacts with Betty Ross. This was the key to Marvel comics during the silver age and what drove the popularity of Marvel characters. These were superheroes that experienced the highs and lows that the readership of these comics also experienced (albeit not in such extreme circumstances). The substance of character development and the foundations for stories were therefore broader. The characters went through a range of emotions over a story arc and this approach to storytelling also provided room for character development.

In the remainder of this chapter, I provide examples of how emotions have been used in developing stories within the Marvel universe during the silver age. In particular, I demonstrate why the experience of emotions and within-person variation was so important to the success of Marvel characters.

THE EXPERIENCE OF EMOTIONS IN MARVEL COMICS

Thomas Scheff argues that the two most powerful primary emotions that drive human experiences are pride and shame. He argues that these are powerful emotions because people are driven to maintain social bonds with others and these emotions protect social bonds.[17] Shame was an initial motivator in the development of many characters in Marvel comics during the silver age. For instance, Steve Rogers's decision to volunteer for the experimental program that transformed him into Captain America was driven by shame at being rejected from army service.[18] Drawing on the simple experience of shame, we have Spider-Man's crime-fighting career emerging from his expression of shame over Peter Parker's role in the death of his Uncle Ben. Indeed, the famous saying "with great power there must also come—great responsibility"[19] is designed to enhance shame of Spider-Man for not using his power to benefit others. Another example of the power of shame emerges in the Hawkeye story line. The character of Hawkeye is developed across a number of stories as an impulsive, self-centered, and egotistical person. There is a continuing story theme of Hawkeye's shame at his constant lack of responsibility within the Avengers, and this shame then motivates his heroic behavior aimed at redeeming himself in others' eyes.[20] Similarly, in creating the Captain America storyline within the Marvel universe, the writers initially teamed Captain America with a teenage sidekick called Bucky Barnes. Much of Captain America's sense of responsibility for looking after people and his fellow team members emerges from the shame and guilt felt by Captain America following the death of Bucky Barnes.[21] As a final example, I note an early Iron Man story in which Tony Stark decides never to shirk his responsibilities as Iron Man after a part-time replacement Iron Man he had employed was injured.[22] Shame, however, is not the only emotion experienced by a broad range of characters. Pride is also evident in many of the silver age revival characters.

Most of Captain America's behavior following his transformation into a supersoldier was driven by pride. Clearly, from his reincarnation in the silver age of comics to join and eventually lead the Avengers,[23] Captain America's primary motivation has been pride in his country or any team with which he has worked. Similarly, Namor the Sub-Mariner expressed pride as the leader of the Atlanteans,[24] Hercules showed pride as the son of Zeus and coming from Olympus,[25] and Thor displayed pride in his status as an Asgardian.[26] This pride was constantly evident during speeches these superheroes made in their battles with villains. Members of various supergroups have also expressed pride. Within early X-Men comics, there are examples of the X-Men showing pride in their school and their teamwork, and their leader Professor Xavier showing pride in the achievements of his protégés.[27] Other characters also have expressed continual pride in their membership of groups, with clear examples being provided by Captain America in the Avengers[28] and the Thing in the Fantastic Four.[29] But Marvel was not just about the simple juxtaposition of pride and shame. Other emotions have also emerged and been used to ground the development of Marvel characters.

In creating his characters, Lee clearly had an understanding of between-person variation and the importance of drawing on that variation in character development. For instance, in his first foray into the Marvel world, Lee developed four distinct characters that were to become the Fantastic Four.[30] An examination of each of the characters from the first issue follows a standard conceptualization of their powers being linked to their dominant personality and accompanying emotional expressions. For instance,

Johnny Storm (the Human Torch) could use flames to fly and as a weapon, which matched his dominant personality of being impulsive (fiery). Reed Richards (Mr. Fantastic) had a flexible body that could stretch into any shape, and this matched his dominant personality trait of having high emotional stability combined with high cognitive flexibility and a superior intelligence, resulting in a calm, rational approach to problem solving. Ben Grimm (the Thing) transformed into an almost invulnerable being with orange, rock-like skin and super strength, which matched his personality of not being particularly approachable. The dramatic change he had undergone resulted in his being confused about his feelings and experiencing a range of emotions from sensitivity to anger. Finally, Susan Storm (the Invisible Girl) had the power to be invisible and to generate a force field that matched her personality of being emotionally stable and empathic resulting in her often being responsible for resolving conflict between Torch and Thing and adding the "human touch" to team decisions (including sympathy for the villains).[31]

The formula established in the first issue of the Fantastic Four[32] was a basic formula of putting contrasting characters in a team together and creating tensions between those characters. This clearly was not new and was used in both the Marvel and the DC universe (e.g., Metal Men[33]). The Marvel difference was that this tension was not just created on the basis of complementing and opposing powers, but also was developed around differing basic personality traits and associated emotional responses. Indeed, this formula was enhanced when Marvel unleashed the power of within-person variation in the Marvel universe. This new direction was clearly expressed in an early Avengers story where Captain America notes "But we are also human beings, with feelings, and emotions."[34] In the next section, I explore the breadth of emotions experienced by one superhero—Spider-Man—and show the importance of within-person variation in developing characters in the Marvel universe during the silver age.

WITHIN-PERSON EMOTIONAL VARIATION

When pitching the Spider-Man series, Stan Lee is reported as saying that he argued with Martin Goodman (the publisher of Marvel at the time) over the character of Spider-Man. "I told him I wanted the character to be a very human guy, someone who makes mistakes, who worries, who gets acne, has trouble with his girlfriend, things like that."[35] Clearly, Lee was interested in portraying a very human character and was determined to ensure Spider-Man was a teenager, even though at the time, the accepted paradigm was that teenagers were always relegated to sidekick roles. By creating Spider-Man as a teenager, Lee had access to a broader range of emotional expressions than one would get from an adult. Spider-Man's emotions were generated by his experiences, and the fact that he was an adolescent meant his experiences were different from those of an adult. Cognitive neuroscientists suggest that during adolescence human beings are generally exposed to a greater range of emotional reactions both due to a lack of experience and as a result of neurophysiological development.[36]

I have already argued that within-person variation was the distinguishing feature of Marvel comics during the silver age of comics. The number of emotions displayed in Marvel during the silver age were diverse, even within one issue. *Amazing Fantasy #15*,[37] the issue that introduced Spider-Man, provides a stark example. Within that issue, readers (and Spider-Man) were exposed to love (his Aunt May and Uncle Ben for Peter Parker), humiliation (Peter Parker's by his classmate Flash Thompson), pride (Peter Parker's, after winning money at the wrestling contest), grief (at learning of

Uncle Ben's death), surprise (finding out the criminal was Uncle Ben's killer), guilt and shame (allowing the criminal who killed Uncle Ben to escape), and anger (seeking revenge for Uncle Ben's death). This range of emotion brought us closer to Peter Parker as a character and made him more believable.

Even the characters that surrounded Spider-Man were susceptible to emotion-driven actions. For instance, in the first issue of the Amazing Spider-Man series,[38] one of the two stories dealt with Spider-Man saving newspaper editor J. Jonah Jameson's son, astronaut John Jameson, from an exploding space capsule. Rather than the gratitude that Spider-Man expects from J. Jonah Jameson, Jameson publishes the first in what will be a long line of "Spider-Man Menace" articles designed to instill fear of Spider-Man into the general public and indeed even into Peter Parker's Aunt May. Jameson's motivation for publishing the "Spider-Man Menace" editorial was the fear that attention would be drawn away from his son's achievements. In other words, this was a decision driven by envy.

Within this same comic book issue, Spider-Man goes through a range of emotions from frustration (throwing his costume against a wall over Uncle Ben's death), worry (over Aunt May's financial situation), confusion (over differential treatment between himself and other superheroes such as the Fantastic Four and Ant Man), anger (when prevented from performing for money because of the timing of John Jameson's space capsule launch), concern (over the imminent crash of the space capsule), elation (at preventing the crash), and trauma (based on the public's reaction to the media campaign that labels Spider-Man as a menace). Although these early issues are dramatic in the range of emotions expressed and experienced, the early issues of *Spider-Man* established a framework for exploring these emotions and behavioral reactions in greater depth in subsequent issues.

Another concept that distinguished Marvel comics from their competitors was the introduction of conflicting emotions experienced by characters in their story lines. Conflicting emotions are defined as the simultaneous experience of two emotions that do not merge with one another.[39] For instance, following the breakup of a relationship we may simultaneously experience feelings of relief/happiness and sadness. In the next section, I examine how these conflicting emotions emerged within characters and within teams, and how this contributed to the breadth of emotional experiences explored in Marvel Comics.

THE EXPERIENCE OF CONFLICTING EMOTIONS IN MARVEL COMICS

Within the Marvel universe there were two sources of conflicting emotion or emotional dissonance.[40] *Emotional dissonance* refers to an experience where the emotions you feel are not in line with the emotions you are expected to express in a given situation.[41] The first source of emotional dissonance was a result of changing allegiances within the Marvel universe, and the second was a result of characters trying to balance their own personal desires against considerations of the greater good (a moral/values dilemma). In terms of changing allegiances, Marvel introduced a number of characters who changed from villains to heroes. Among them are the Scarlet Witch and Quicksilver, mutants who had been members of the Brotherhood of Evil Mutants.[42] After the Brotherhood were defeated by the X-Men, Scarlet Witch and Quicksilver declared that they no longer owed a debt of gratitude to Magneto (the leader of a group the Brotherhood of Evil Mutants and an arch enemy of the X-Men) and stated that they regretted joining him. The Scarlet Witch and Quicksilver subsequently joined the Avengers[43] and constantly dealt with emotional issues around split loyalties. Similarly, Hawkeye, who initially was cast as a villain in a number of stories, had a bad experience that made him rethink his criminal activities[44] and join the Avengers as a hero.[45] Other characters that had similar changes of heart include Namor the Sub-Mariner and the Silver Surfer, who both started off as villains in *The Fantastic Four* and eventually changed to become heroes in their own series. For instance, in outlining the origins of the Silver Surfer,[46] one scene reveals the Silver Surfer remembering the pact he made with Galactus (an omnipotent being who can restructure matter at a molecular level but requires great energy to do so, with the preferred energy source being planets). In this recollection, the Silver Surfer agrees to find planets for Galactus to feed on in order to prevent Galactus from feeding on the Silver Surfer's planet. The emotional dissonance experienced by the Silver Surfer (between guilt at dooming other planets and relief at saving his own planet) was clear in the story line. There are also the villains that were misunderstood and moved on later to become heroes (e.g., The Inhumans[47]). The situations these characters find themselves in are ripe for exploring the experience of conflicting emotions and ambivalence, and the story lines developed took advantage of this.

The second area in which Marvel introduced conflicting emotions and emotional dissonance was in stories that dealt with superheroes considering their own desires and juxtaposing these against the greater good. Previous examples I have outlined include Spider-Man's conflicting emotions over earning money as opposed to saving people,[48] and Iron Man's conflict over his risking his life even when he isn't appreciated—or he is even maligned.[49]

Taking another example from a different set of characters, we see that the writers clearly understood how to use conflicting emotions within story lines. For instance, in *Avengers #25*, the Scarlet

Witch ponders her attraction to Captain America and thinks "am I confusing pity with the dawning of love?"[50] Clearly, this is a complex interaction that engages the reader to make a distinction between the warm feelings aroused by pity and the warm feelings aroused by love.

To this point, I have mainly focused at the individual level on single characters' experience of emotions in the Marvel universe. To complete my argument about the centrality of emotion, I want to explain how Marvel stories explored the impact of emotions on teams or at the group level.

EMOTIONS IN TEAMS

An examination of emotions that emerged within Marvel teams confirms the importance of emotion within the development of those teams. To demonstrate this it is easiest to start with how teams were conceived and developed within the DC universe, in which a prototypical superhero group was the Justice League of America (JLA).[51] For this team, the focus of the story was the combined powers of the superheroes and how these superpowered combinations could be used to defeat villains. Often a weakness was identified in one hero, and this weakness was compensated for by the strength of another hero. In other words, these super group stories were character driven. Another group that was the epitome of this genre was the Legion of Superheroes.[52] Unlike most supergroups, which seemed to have limits to the size of their membership, the Legion had massive numbers (Mon-el, Brainiac 5, Invisible Girl, Colossal Boy, Bouncing Boy, Triplicate Girl, Ultra Boy, Cosmic Boy, Lightning Lad, Saturn Girl, Star Boy, Shrinking Violet, Superboy, and Supergirl, to name a few), and the story line often involved new members being tested to join the group and either succeeding or failing.[53] The issue here is that the writers used this range of characters to sustain an interesting story line. Thus, rather than take the time to develop the personality of the Legion characters to make them more engaging, the writers decided to constantly introduce new characters as a method of diversifying the story lines.

Researchers who study teams examine dynamics in groups, and have found an inverse relationship between group size and performance.[54] That is, the larger the group, the less it achieves. On this basis the number of characters in the Legion made it an unsustainable group. Large groups generally suffer from conflict and volatile emotional expressions between members based on the conflicting goals that each person brings to the group. This conflict affects both team communication and goal setting.[55] None of these effects were evident in Legion stories, as the writers would primarily focus on a couple of different characters in each story and each story would then explore how these heroes' powers complemented one another. The central issue here is that within the DC universe (whether we examine the JLA or the Legion), supergroup stories were character driven.

In contrast, in the Marvel universe teams were generally kept to a reasonable size, and membership was generally consistent to allow for a greater depth of interaction and character development. This enabled the emotional reactions of these characters to be explored in these groups. For instance, The Fantastic Four was a small group, allowing each of the characters to be considered both as individuals and as members of the team. From their first issue,[56] the Fantastic Four has been a group consisting of family members and close friends that were thrust into an unusual situation. They were not only trying to understand and cope with their developing powers, they were also coping with living together as a group. Typical story lines generally had emotions flowing between the Thing and Torch—teasing and banter that inevitably resulted in both verbal and physical conflict.[57] Sometimes the conflict was playful, at other times serious.

At the same time, within the Fantastic Four adventure story lines, other relationship-oriented story lines emerged. This was exemplified by the romance between Mr. Fantastic and the Invisible Girl. This wasn't the romance of Hollywood (or Lois and Clark)—there were stumbles and falls and disagreements and attractions with one notable segment where Mr. Fantastic admonishes the Invisible Girl to "stop acting like a wife."[58]

Similarly, The Avengers during the silver age (Captain America, Thor, Ant-Man/Giant Man, the Wasp, and Iron Man) were always uncomfortable alliances of superheroes who, at times, could not stand each other and often agonized over their membership. So in the early days Ant-Man/Giant Man was seen as creating conflict in the group. In later incarnations of the Avengers, the squeaky clean and goal focused Captain America was joined by former villains Hawkeye, Scarlet Witch, and Quicksilver, who all had conflicting loyalties and volatile personalities.[59] Again, interest was enhanced by ensuring a diverse range of personalities and reactions were available for the story writers to draw on.

The final aspect of group emotion that Marvel explored was group *emotional contagion*. Emotional contagion is a process in which individuals mimic the emotions of others and in doing so end up actually experiencing those emotions.[60] A good example of this phenomenon is the Sons of Serpents story arc in *The Avengers*,[61] where the caption reads "Within minutes the swelling crowd turns into an enraged, uncomprehending mob—confused, blinded by emotion and seething with hate—!" This type of simple emotional contagion was a factor in many Marvel stories and was documented by psychology researchers through Robert Zimbardo's Stanford experiments conducted in 1971, an experiment that showed the contagious effect of human behavior.[62]

Emotional contagion effects also arose within superhero groups, particularly the contagion of positive emotions. Examples of this include Captain America's constant calls for the Avengers to hold together in the face of overwhelming odds, which was intended to encourage enthusiasm and optimism among his team. At the same time, Captain America's constant displays of bravery and optimism in taking on larger and more powerful foes were seen as a positive model of expected behavior to other members of the Avengers. Similarly, Professor X encouraged positivity and caring among the X-Men, enabling them to act as a team in facing their enemies. This approach is in line with research that demonstrates the importance of positive emotion in group cohesion.[63] In this case, Professor X could not demonstrate positivity through actions as he was wheelchair bound and therefore had to encourage it through speeches and coaching.

CONCLUSION

In summary, stories in the silver age of Marvel comics demonstrate a sophisticated understanding of the role of emotions within individuals and within groups and how emotions drive human behavior. Stories were based on complex character development that resulted in emotional dissonance for individual heroes as they balanced their own desires with that of the group, but also explored the nature of simple emotional contagion in groups.

Clearly, the silver age of comics was important in developing a new paradigm of characters that had broader emotional experiences. Indeed the real contribution of Marvel within this period is demonstrated in the fact that readers of comics are now being asked to engage with real issues such as drug use.[64] As I noted earlier, I suggest this phenomenon can be traced back to Marvel during the silver age through its adoption of emotion in story lines and in character development. In particular, these early Marvel stories are enhanced by their writers' use of psychological theory around the two-factor model of emotion[65] and situational within-person variation in behaviors.[66]

NOTES

1. Smith R. W. (2009, October 12) Comics 101—What is the silver age of comics? *EzineArticles.* Accessed January 27, 2011, at http://ezinearticles.com/?Comics-101—What-is-the-Silver-Age-of-Comics?&id=3077462.
2. Kanigher, R., & Infantino, C. (1956). The Flash. *Showcase*, Vol. 1, No. 4, DC Comics.
3. Broome, J., & Kane, G. (1959). Green Lantern. *Showcase*, Vol. 1, No. 22, DC Comics.
4. Fox, G. F., & Kane, G. (1961). Inside the Atom. *Showcase*, Vol. 1, No. 35, DC Comics.
5. Smith (2009).
6. Lee, S., & Kirby, J. (1961). The Fantastic Four. *The Fantastic Four*, Vol. 1, No. 1, Marvel Comics Group.
7. Lee, S., & Ditko, S. (1962). Spider-Man. *Amazing Fantasy*, Vol. 1, No. 15, Marvel Comics Group.
8. Lee, S., & Kirby, J. (1963). X-Men. *The X-Men*, Vol. 1, No. 1, Marvel Comics Group.
9. Lee, S., & Kirby, J. (1963). The coming of the avengers. *The Avengers*, Vol. 1, No. 1, Marvel Comics Group.
10. Schachter, S., & Singer, J. (1962). Cognitive, social, and physiological determinants of emotional state. *Psychological Review, 69,* 379–399.
11. Mischel, W., & Shoda, Y. (1995). A cognitive-affective system theory of personality: Reconceptualizing situations, dispositions, dynamics, and invariance in personality structure. *Psychological Review, 102,* 246–268.
12. Schachter & Singer (1962).

13. See Cervone, D. (2005). Personality architecture: Within person structures and processes. *Annual Review of Psychology, 56,* 423–452.
14. Broome, J., & Infantino, C. (1964). The mystery of the menacing mask. *Detective Comics*, Vol. 1, No. 327, DC Comics.
15. Broome & Kane (1959). Green Lantern.
16. Mischel & Shoda (1995).
17. Scheff, T. J. (1990). *Microsociology: Discourse, emotion, and social structure.* Chicago: University of Chicago Press.
18. Simon, J., & Kirby, J. (1941). Meet Captain America, *Captain America Comics*, Vol. 1, No. 1.
19. Lee & Ditko (1962). Spider-Man.
20. Lee, S., & Heck, D. (1966). This power unleashed. *The Avengers*, Vol. 1, No. 29, Marvel Comics Group.
21. Thomas, R., & Buscema, J. (1968). Death be not proud. *The Avengers*, Vol. 1, No. 56, Marvel Comics Group.
22. Goodwin, S., & Tuska, G. (1970). Death must follow. *The Invincible Iron Man*, Vol. 1, No. 22, Marvel Comics Group.
23. Lee, S., & Kirby, J. (1964). Captain America joins… The Avengers. *The Avengers*, Vol. 1, No. 4, Marvel Comics Group.
24. Thomas R., & Buscema, J. (1968). Who strikes for Atlantis? *Prince Namor the Sub-Mariner*, Vol. 1, No. 4, Marvel Comics Group.
25. Thomas, R., & Heck, D. (1967). In our midst… an immortal. *The Avengers*, Vol. 1, No. 38, Marvel Comics Group.
26. Lee, S., & Kirby. J. (1966). Whom the Gods would destroy. *The Mighty Thor*, Vol. 1, No. 126, Marvel Comics Group.
27. Lee, S., & Kirby, J. (1964). The Angel is trapped. *The X-Men*, Vol. 1, No. 5, Marvel Comics Group.
28. Thomas, R., & Heck, D. (1966). The light that failed. *The Avengers*, Vol. 1, No. 35, Marvel Comics Group.
29. Lee, S., & Kirby, J. (1964). We have to fight the X-Men! *The Fantastic Four*, Vol. 1, No. 28, Marvel Comics Group.
30. Lee, S., & Kirby, J. (1961). The Fantastic Four. *The Fantastic Four*, Vol. 1, No. 1, Marvel Comics Group.

31. Lee & Kirby (1961). The Fantastic Four.
32. Lee & Kirby (1961). The Fantastic Four.
33. Kanigher, R., & Andru, R. (1962). Metal Men, *Showcase*, No. 37, DC Comics.
34. Lee & Heck (1966). This power unleashed.
35. Theakston, G. (2002). *The Steve Ditko Reader.* Brooklyn, NY: Pure Imagination, p. 12.
36. Burnett, S., Bird, G., Moll, J., Frith, C., & Blakemore, S.J. (2009). Development during adolescence of the neural processing of social emotion. *Journal of Cognitive Neuroscience, 21*(9), 1736–1750.
37. Lee & Ditko (1962). Spider-Man.
38. Lee & Ditko (1962). Spider-Man.
39. Larsen, J. T., McGraw, A. P., & Cacioppo, J. T. (2001). Can people feel happy and sad at the same time? *Journal of Personality and Social Psychology, 81,* 684–696.
40. Hochschild, A. R. (1983). *The managed heart: Commercialization of human feeling.* Berkeley: University of California Press.
41. Hochschild (1983).
42. Lee, S., & Kirby, J. (1965). The old order changeth. *The Avengers*, Vol. 1, No. 16, Marvel Comics Group.
43. Lee & Kirby (1965). The old order changeth.
44. Lee, S., & Heck, D. (1965). Hawkeye and the new Black Widow strike again! *Tales of Suspense*, Vol. 1, No. 64, Marvel Comics Group.
45. Lee & Kirby (1965). The old order changeth.
46. Lee, S., & Buscema, J. (1968). The origin of the Silver Surfer. *The Silver Surfer*, Vol. 1, No. 1, Marvel Comics Group.
47. Lee, S., & Kirby, J. (1966). Those who would destroy us. *The Fantastic Four*, Vol. 1, No. 46, Marvel Comics Group.
48. Lee & Ditko (1962). Spider-Man.
49. Goodwin & Tuska (1970). Death must follow.
50. Lee, S., & Heck, D. (1966). Enter Dr. Doom. *The Avengers*, Vol. 1, No. 25, Marvel Comics Group.

51. Fox, G. F., & Sekowsky, M. (1960). World of no return. *Justice League of America*, Vol. 1, No. 1, DC Comics.
52. Binder, O., & Plastino, A. (1958). The legion of super-heroes. *Adventure Comics*, No. 247, DC Comics.
53. See Siegel, J., & Mooney, J. (1960). The three super-heroes. *Action Comics*, Vol. 1, No. 276, DC Comics.
54. Latane, B., Williams, K., & Harkins, S. (1979). Many hands make light the work: The causes and consequences of social loafing. *Journal of Personality and Social Psychology, 37,* 822–832.
55. Jordan, P. J., & Troth, A. C. (2004). Managing emotions during team problem solving: Emotional intelligence and conflict resolution. *Human Performance, 17*(2), 195–218.
56. Lee & Kirby (1961). The Fantastic Four.
57. For an example of an argument between the Torch, the Thing, and the Invisible Girl, see Lee & Kirby (1966), Those who would destroy us,
58. Lee, S., & Kirby, J. (1966). Beware the hidden land. *The Fantastic Four*, Vol. 1, No. 47, Marvel Comics Group.
59. Lee & Kirby (1965). The old order changeth.
60. Barsade, S. G. (2002). The ripple effect: Emotional contagion and its influence on group behavior. *Administrative Science Quarterly, 47,* 644–675.
61. Lee, S., & Heck, D. (1966). The sign of the serpent. *The Avengers*, Vol. 1, No. 32, Marvel Comics Group.
62. Zimbardo, P. G. (2007). *The Lucifer effect: Understanding how good people turn evil.* New York: Random House.
63. Lawler, E. J., Thye, S. R., & Yoon, J. (2000). Emotion and group cohesion in productive exchange. *American Journal of Sociology, 106,* 616–657.
64. O'Neil, D., & Adams, N. (1971). Snowbirds don't fly. *Green Lantern / Green Arrow*, Vol. 1, No. 85, DC Comics.
65. Schachter & Singer (1962).
66. Mischel & Shoda (1995).

FIVE

The Effects of Superhero Sagas on Our Gendered Selves

Elizabeth Behm-Morawitz and Hillary Pennell

EDITOR'S NOTE

Female superheroes are powerful women yet they are also sexualized and thus in a sense disempowered. Though all superhero bodies tend to be unrealistic and idealized, male superheroes are not sexualized in an analogous way to female superheroes. Do the gendered roles and bodies of superheroes affect us? As you'll see in this essay by Elizabeth Behm-Morawitz and Hillary Pennell, the answer is "yes." This duo of authors is well prepared to tackle the complexities of representations of gender in superhero stories based on their research questions about the effects of gender and stereotypes in various media, including video games.

—Robin S. Rosenberg

Since the emergence of *Superman* in the 1930s, superheroes have dominated comic book narratives, successfully crossing over into other forms of media. Although the popularity of comic book superheroes and their stories have been in flux over the years, recently their adoration has been reinvigorated through big-budget cinema blockbusters like *X-Men* (2000), *Spider-Man* (2002), *Batman Begins* (2005), *Superman Returns* (2006), *Iron-Man* (2008), and *The Incredible Hulk* (2008), to name a few. Superheroes and their fantastical lives draw the youthful moviegoing demographic, appeal to the nostalgic older audiences, and present well-established characters and story lines with which audiences connect. But what is it about superheroes that appeals to our gendered selves—our lives experienced as boys, girls, men, and women? This chapter argues that superhero texts do not merely entertain; they may have real-world implications for how we construct gender-related identities, attitudes, and beliefs. We examine the psychological appeal of superheroes as well as the potential effects of identification with these extraordinary characters on our gendered selves.

THE APPEAL OF SUPER(GENDERED)HEROES

At the most basic level, superhero sagas impact our lives by fulfilling an entertainment need. Fans of the superhero genre are typically fans because they *enjoy* superhero narratives, characters, and/or art. Entertainment media, in general, serve an important purpose by appealing to some of our most basic emotions.[1] Fans' enjoyment of superhero sagas results in feelings of joy and happiness, helps to manage their mood state, and peaks their interest. Psychology research[2] suggests that *novel stimuli*—like the extraordinary superheroes, superheroines, their nemeses, and their stories—interest us because of their distinctive newness.[3] Though many forms of entertainment media present novel stimuli, it stands to reason that superhero sagas have unique appeal in that they offer up an escape into fantastical worlds. Unlike many other genres, superhero stories appeal to the desire to inhabit a fantasy world rich with novel and fantastical beings, places, and events. The superhuman elements of superhero sagas present audiences with stories that are centered on stimuli unique from real life.

At the same time, these superhero stories are appealing because they provide us with *familiar narratives*,[4] which increase our enjoyment with characters and plot elements we understand. The often-formulaic superhero story may provide novel stimuli, but in a somewhat predictable pattern that is inviting and comfortable. For example, themes of war, love, morality, and personal identity struggles, which have basis in our experienced realities, permeate superhero sagas.

One very familiar narrative element is the hypergendering (or supergendering) of characters in superhero sagas. Scholars and media critics alike have analyzed gender in superhero texts and agree that these beloved stories most often depict characters who typify conventional gender norms. Male characters are typically hypermasculine and female characters are most often hyperfeminine and/or hypersexualized in the superhero world.[5] In particular, male superhero characters fill stereotypical gender roles that epitomize idealizations of masculinity. Male superheroes are constructed in ways that emphasize strength and power to a heightened, superhuman degree that speaks to Western ideas about masculinity and manhood. These superheroes have bodies that are muscled and sculpted; they perform feats of strength and heroism that exemplify the masculine role of the protector and fearless leader.

Additionally, the construction of female characters in superhero sagas underscores these messages about masculinity. When women are included in superhero stories, they tend to be love interests and/or victims in need of rescue by male superheroes. Their abilities are stripped from them, whereas their bodies are the primary focus. The largest recurring role for these damsels in distress (e.g., Mary Jane in *Spider-Man* and Betty Ross in *Incredible Hulk*) is that of a victim in need of saving by her male rescuer. These images of women fit with stereotypical conventions of femininity and serve to support normative messages of masculinity, positioning men to be largely in control and capable. However, superhero stories take a familiar gender narrative and transform it into a supergendered narrative, with hypermuscular male heroes and hypersexualized female victims, glorifying traditional gender roles.

A notable exception to this portrayal of females in superhero texts is the relatively infrequent but powerful representation of the female superhero, which both resists and conforms to familiar gender conventions. On the one hand, female superheroes (e.g., Wonder Woman and Storm) offer up a much more empowered and strong picture of a woman in comparison to the typical female depiction in superhero stories. On the other hand, these characters conform to gendered stereotypes by being presented in a hypersexualized manner. The focus on their bodies and sexuality may position them primarily as objects of desire in ways that are not as typical of male superheroes. The media have a long history of focusing on the youth, beauty, and sexuality of female characters more so than male characters. Thus, the sexualization of female superheroes fits within this familiar gendered media narrative, while the more masculine characterizations of these heroines push the boundaries of normative gender representations.

Female fans in particular may find female superheroes to be appealing because they offer up a rare image of the mediated female—a woman with superhuman strength who is powerful and capable of doing the rescuing—instead of *being* rescued. Simultaneously, these heroines appeal to us in the way that they do not deviate so far from traditional gender norms, that is, by maintaining a focus on their body and sexuality. Indeed, research suggests that the female superhero is most appealing to audiences when her masculine traits are balanced with familiar feminine values, such as compassion.[6] This combination of the masculine and hyperfeminine creates a female superhero who is indeed novel, because of her demonstration of masculine strength, yet who also reflects the familiar practice of the sexualization of women in the media.

In sum, audiences may enjoy the narrative familiarity of the supergendering of men and women in superhero sagas. Yet these gendered messages are made special by exaggerating masculine and feminine traits of characters in superhero narratives. This provides fans with the ideal entertainment offering—a story that is both familiar and novel. Most of us are socialized into accepting, to some degree—or at the very least recognizing—culturally dominant gender norms. Superhero sagas make sense to us and appeal to the socially constructed view of our gendered selves.

MORE THAN JUST ENTERTAINMENT

As we've explored in our analysis, it is certainly true that superhero stories are entertaining as they target and trigger positive emotional experiences for fans and appeal to the imagination in a way that can be understood in terms of real (gendered) human experiences. But superhero sagas also affect our lives in less obvious ways beyond simple entertainment.

Before we examine each of these types of media effects in turn in relation to superhero texts and audiences, let's understand how these legendary characters may help to fulfill relationship and identity needs for fans. The research on *media identification* and *parasocial interaction*[7] (i.e., relationships that media users form with media characters) helps to explain how fans form meaningful connections with superheroes. Though the parasocial relationships people develop with superheroes are one-sided, they feel quite real. This, as well as fans' identification or ability to relate to superhero characters, provides a foundation for understanding how superheroes may affect how people perceive themselves as well as others.

Media Identification and Interaction with Superheroes

One well-established area of media research explores the processes of how, and to what degree, people identify with and come to relate to media characters. Generally, people may form a bond with media characters they like and desire to become more like these media personas (i.e., "wishful identification").[8] A fan may form a *parasocial* (one-sided) relationship[9] with a media figure and treat it as if it were a real relationship. These experiences are correlated. The more someone identifies with a superhero character, the more likely he or she is to form a parasocial relationship, and vice versa.

Given that the media industry is dominated by male writers, artists, producers, directors, and critics, it is not surprising that most superhero characters are male. And despite the increased visibility of female superhero fans,[10] the target audience of the superhero genre is still boys and men. To appeal to this male audience, superhero stories centering on male superheroes are most prevalent. The industry assertions that boys and men prefer male rather than female characters—thereby explaining why most characters are male—may not be far off the mark. Past research[11] demonstrates that boys are most likely to identify with male superheroes, whereas girls may identify with either female or male superheroes. However, this should not be taken to mean that boys and men do not respond well to female superheroes. It would not be uncommon for boys and men to develop parasocial relationships with female superheroes, even though they likely more closely identify with the male characters.

Whether one identifies and/or forms a parasocial relationship with a male or female superhero character, this process is not all that different from the formation of real-life social interactions.[12] The psychology of the appeal of superheroes can partly be explained by the phenomenon of fans getting to know superhero characters in ways that are similar to how they form attachments to friends, neighbors, and loved ones. In turn, as fans get to know superheroes, they can develop feelings of similarity, empathy, idolization, and loyalty to these media characters—in a fashion similar to the feelings they develop with actual social others. We see this most obviously evidenced at fan conventions and online, where fans express their deep attachments to superhero characters. These characters are more than fictional creations; they are perceived as being real confidants, friends, and/or potential lovers.

At one time, parasocial interaction with superheroes would have been considered psychopathological, but today, scholars of communication and psychology view these relationships with mediated persons as perfectly normal. These parasocial relationships provide real emotional and social experiences that fulfill entertainment, network, and affective needs for fans.

Though male fans have many more opportunities to identify with gender-similar superheroes than do female fans, we would like to consider the special case of the potential identification and parasocial interaction of female fans with the female superhero (or the superheroine).

The Empowering Superheroine?

Looking past entertainment, media and psychology research suggests that superheroes may influence the ways we think about ourselves and others. It is known that people learn about gender norms and expectations from exposure to media. More specifically, gendered media portrayals influence individuals' self-concept,[13] beliefs about traditional gender roles,[14] gender stereotyping,[15] body esteem and eating disordered behaviors,[16] and self-objectification (i.e., the view of one's body as an object for others' enjoyment).[17]

It can be argued that many of the superheroines like DC's Wonder Woman and Catwoman[18] and Marvel's Storm and Elektra[19] are empowering characters. These characters are physically strong, athletic, capable, authoritative, and intelligent.

They are tough and beautiful. Although their sex appeal may be seen as objectification of the female body, it may also be constructed as empowering by showing distain for traditional feminine modesty.

These characters also showcase powerful abilities and engage in aggressive behaviors that are not typically associated with women. For example, Catwoman has a deadly whip, a makeup compact and perfume that can render her opponents unconscious, claw gloves for maximum damage when in combat mode, and of course the ability to cat-apult and propel herself over great distances while gently landing on her feet.[20] Wonder Woman has a tiara that can be used as a boomerang, bracelets that can deflect bullets, a golden lasso that can extract the truth and erase memories, and sandals for dimensional travel, not to mention superstrength and immortality.[21] The women of *X-Men* all display great powers. Storm showcases great fighting aptitude as well the ability to manipulate the weather. Rogue has the ability to absorb others' strength, memories, and abilities, potentially killing them simply through her touch. Mystique is an agile fighter and expert in martial arts with the ability to alter her shape and mimic the physical form of any human being or mutant. Susan Storm Richards, a member of The Fantastic Four and also known as the Invisible Woman, has the power of invisibility; she is also able to project powerful force fields of energy that she can use for offense or defense. All of these superheroines physically dominate and excel in activities that are normally associated with masculinity.

As such, female fans may develop wishful identification with superheroines, resulting in a desire to be more like them. Girls and women may feel empowered through the identification and parasocial interaction experienced with these phenomenal female characters. At fan conventions, a woman may dress as a beloved superheroine and feel pride and ownership over this media character. In a gendered franchise that largely sidelines women and girls in superhero stories, superheroines may provide a unique opportunity for female fans to feel empowered rather than disempowered when participating in the superhero genre.

It is true that these superheroines have broken down gender barriers; however, the potential for superheroines to be empowering for women and girls may be limited by these heroines' objectification in superhero texts and their subordination to male characters. Although at times female superheroes have powers seemingly equal to their male counterparts, the male superheroes are often more likely to be in greater positions of authority, like that of a mentor. Superhero stories may construct a superheroine as dependent on a male character by having her rely on a man to guide or train her to develop her skills. For example, Marvel's Elektra is drugged and kidnapped in order to be reeducated about the misguided choices she has made in her past. It is a man, Jeremy Locke, who teaches Elektra how to use her powers for good. In the DC comic *Batgirl*, Batman plays the part of Batgirl's mentor, telling her what missions to go on, evaluating her performance, and giving her advice.

Although superheroines' powers are not always weaker than superheroes, they often are depicted as having less control over them, needing help of the male heroes/mentors to guide them and their abilities. While outwardly Dr. Jean Grey of the *X-Men* film series possesses more powerful abilities than her male counterparts—telepathic and telekinetic powers that can be used at a subatomic level—making her the most powerful and most dangerous mutant, she cannot control them. Eventually, she turns against her fellow teammates, even killing her beloved mentor Professor Charles Xavier when she loses control of her abilities.

This dichotomous representation of superheroines as being extraordinary women yet sexualized and less super than their male counterparts muddies the potential for these characters to be empowering media figures. No doubt, women and girls do feel empowered by these characters, at times; however they have also objected to the gendered treatment of female characters in superhero sagas. Specifically, female fans have openly expressed their disappointment and anger at the sexualization and victimization of women in superhero narratives. Blogs, such as "Women in Refrigerators," are written by female fans who express a love for comic books but a disdain for the stereotypical and gendered violent treatment (e.g., rape) of women in these superhero stories.

Gender Stereotyping and Fan Resistance

A gender stereotype is generally defined as "a set of beliefs about what it means to be female or male. Gender stereotypes include information about physical appearance, attitudes and interests, psychological traits, social relations, and occupations.[22] The media serve as one source of learning about gender roles, and research[23] suggests that exposure to stereotypical gender portrayals, such as those found in superhero sagas, is linked to gender stereotyping by fans in the real world.

In addition to media identification and parasocial interaction, the effects of gender representation in superhero texts may be understood through the lens of media stereotyping. Scholars have systematically examined the effects of exposure to gender stereotypes (and counterstereotypes) in entertainment media on people's real-world judgments of women and men.

Of particular interest here are the effects of exposure to sexual and body-related stereotypes of women and girls in the media. Monique Ward and Kimberly Friedman experimentally examined the effects on adolescents of exposure to portrayals of women as sex objects; teens were more likely to report stereotypical gender role beliefs and to condone such treatment of women.[24] This has clear implications for female superhero fans, since women in the superhero genre are most often objectified, using sexuality as the focus of their characters, and are not typically offered as much complexity in the story line as are male characters.[25]

You may notice an apparent contradiction. On the one hand, earlier we proposed that female superheroes may be empowering via the power and strength they exhibit; on the other hand, female superheroes—at least as they are now portrayed—may be disempowering due to the objectification of these characters. But research suggests the mere sexualization of powerful female characters may negate the potential positive effects of such characters. For example, research[26] examined the effects of playing a highly sexualized versus less sexualized version of Lara Croft in *Tomb Raider: Legend* and found that playing the sexualized Croft resulted in college students' judging women more negatively in the real world. Thus, even though Croft is a strong, intelligent, and powerful character, when sexualized, she is not so empowering. She may trigger gender stereotypical thoughts about women. This particular investigation looked at the short-term effects of superheroine video game play in a lab, but research suggests that the impact of sexualized superheroines might be even greater for heavy consumers of the genre. In other words, avid fans may be more likely to develop attitudes and beliefs about women that are in line with gender stereotypes in superhero stories than a person who, say, watches the occasional superhero Blockbuster film.

When considering how male superhero characters are depicted, it stands to reason that the hypermasculine representations may likewise result in greater adherence to traditional notions of what it means to be a man. Specifically, superhero fans may adopt more gender traditional attitudes and beliefs, expecting men to act as protectors, heroes, enforcers, athletes, and intellectuals. Certainly, media narratives and characters typically play only a small role in how our gender-related attitudes and beliefs develop, but it is a measurable one and has been demonstrated to have at least short-term effects on real-world gender role beliefs. Thus, scholars and fans should not dismiss the potential for superhero sagas to impart gender stereotypes to audiences.

However, not all portrayals of gender in superhero texts are gender typical in nature. Although less frequent, superhero sagas sometimes portray men and women in roles that do not conform to traditional gender role stereotypes. This is potentially positive, because stereotypes are limiting and can constrain personal and social identity. Thus, when superhero stories depict the physically dominant female and the sensitive male, we should remember that media research[27] suggests such portrayals may help to counter stereotypical notions about how women and men should act. This in turn offers superhero audiences more space to develop their own sense of gender as well as break down gender stereotypes that may be used to negatively judge others who do not embody them.

Superhero texts may do more than simply entertain: they may influence gender-related beliefs and attitudes that impact on how we view men and women. Though this phenomenon is not unique to the superhero genre—in fact, it relates to all media offerings—there is a reason why superhero stories may be considered a special case. Not only do superhero stories present some alternative gender models (i.e., superheroines), but the fan community makes the genre unique. The intensely loyal, invested, and active community of superhero fans[28] has a long history of reenacting the gender roles communicated through superhero stories through fan activities such as role-playing and fan fiction. This replaying and negotiating of the gendered messages in superhero texts offers a more complex picture of the relationship between media exposure and gender stereotyping. Indeed, cultural studies research[29] demonstrates that fans do not necessarily internalize mediated gender stereotypes, and may routinely engage in practices to resist them. Thus, we conclude that the relationship between superhero stories and gender stereotyping is not a simple one—superheroes have the potential to both reinforce and subvert gender stereotypes.

Self-Concept: How Super Am I?

Beyond influencing how we think about others, superhero texts may influence how we think about ourselves. Superhero stories may have a psychological effect on the self-concept. More specifically, self-esteem (i.e., evaluation of self-worth or importance) and self-efficacy (i.e., belief in one's abilities to accomplish things) may be affected by superhero stories. From the framework of social comparison theory,[30] engagement in upward social comparison with superhero figures may result in the view of the self as inadequate in comparison to these extraordinary beings.[31] Superheroes are gifted (see Rosenberg and Winner's chapter in this volume), powerful superhumans, and when we compare ourselves to these media models, research suggests that this may have a negative impact on self-esteem and self-efficacy when we find that we do not measure up.

Further, media research suggests that the female self-concept, in particular, may be negatively impacted by exposure to superhero sagas. This largely stems from the portrayal of female characters in superhero stories as sexualized, victimized, and objectified, as discussed earlier. In fact, as women internalize the communicated standards of the female body in the media, they generally have lower self-esteem and self-efficacy.[32]

Similarly, this process may also lower self-efficacy in female fans, despite the physical and intellectual power of the characters. Researchers[33] found that playing Tomb Raider's *sexualized* Lara Croft lowered self-efficacy in young adult female players. So although superheroines demonstrate superior strength and intelligence, their objectification may negate positive effects on self-concept and lessen girls' and women's confidence in their own abilities to succeed.

Conversely, there is potential for superheroes to engender positive feelings of the self. This is likely to occur when audiences find superheroes to be inspiring figures with whom they can relate and wish to emulate. The heroic nature of male and female superheroes and fans' connection to these characters through identification and parasocial interaction may inspire confidence in one's own ability to help others and to persevere in life. In one study, Leif Nelson and Michael Norton[34] asked a group of college students to think about and describe the characteristics of a superhero. The researchers then compared these participants' intention to help others with another group of college students who did not engage in the superhero description activity. The results of the experiment showed that the students who were asked to think about superheroes reported higher intention to help those in need than did the students who were not asked to think about a superhero. Three months later, the effect still held, suggesting that superhero stories may have lasting influence on positive behavior and our beliefs in our own abilities to act heroically.

Superbodies: Effects on Body-Related Beliefs and Behaviors

Women in superhero stories generally conform to what is called the *curvaceously thin* female body ideal, and male superheroes are portrayed with the ideal *V-shape* (broad, muscular chest and shoulders with a trim waist) that is so prevalent in mainstream US media. However, as we argued earlier, these are exaggerated versions of the ideal male and female bodies that are not found in many other media and this "anatomical exaggeration" (p. 354) of male and female bodies—superbodies—in superhero texts reinforces the dichotomy between the masculine and feminine body.[35]

DC's Batman, for example, has very visible muscle definition on the stomach, arm, and thigh regions. Batman's body is disproportionate, with his waist and head being much smaller than would realistically appear in combination with his rippled muscular body. In fact, the extremely large size of Batman's (and most male superheroes') muscles are only matched in the real world by the most extreme male body builders who work hard to manufacture a body that most men could not achieve.

For female superheroes, a thin body (with no visible body fat) and large breasts make up the ideal body, typically only attainable in the real world through surgical enhancement.[36] Perhaps it is not surprising that superheroines—who are, after all, *extraordinary* by nature—embody this nearly impossible standard of beauty. This trend began as far back as the 1940s with the superheroine Wonder Woman, who in the comic book wore the unforgettable red bustier, accentuating her large breasts and small waist, and blue shorts with white stars emphasizing her buttocks and long legs. More recently, Tomb Raider's popular animated video game heroine Lara Croft was given such large breasts and small frame that if she were a real person with those same anatomical dimensions, she would literally tip over from being too top heavy. Though this body type is largely unattainable for women and girls, this female superbody is still used to judge women's bodies in the real world.

Social scientific research[37] has demonstrated that exposure to such idealized media images of female bodies may lower girls' and women's satisfaction with their own bodies and increase disordered eating behaviors. Such effects have been found for both children and adults. Media images of the female body may have negative effects on body esteem beginning even at a young age and continue throughout much of a women's life. For boys and men, idealized imagery of the male body in the media has been linked to being dissatisfied with one's own muscles, problematic exercising, and the intention to use steroids.[38]

One of the most potentially damaging outcomes of consuming these idealized images in superhero stories is self-objectification. Whereas body esteem is about satisfaction with your own appearance, self-objectification refers to the tendency for a person to place great importance on the appearance of her body and to view the body from a third-person perspective—being most concerned about how the body appears to others.[39] A person with a high level of self-objectification would view her worth as intrinsically tied to how well her physical appearance conforms to others' ideals of beauty. In self-objectification, the body is viewed as an object that exists for the pleasure of others. In superhero films, this is purposefully developed through various camera techniques. Although the objectification of women's bodies is not new to film, this is especially prevalent in superhero films. The camera pans up a woman's body or focuses on certain parts, usually the chest and legs, and the audience is positioned to her body voyeuristically. Showing a woman's body fragmented into parts communicates to the audience that she is not a person, but rather an object to be viewed. In the film *Spider-Man* (2002), for example, Mary Jane's body was objectified by using angling and panning techniques like shooting from the waist up, cutting off her lower body to emphasize her torso and large chest, as well as using angled shots to peer down her open shirt or up her short skirt.

Indeed, it is not only the female body that is objectified in visual representations of superheroes. The male superhero is also subject to the audience's gaze, though the male body is costumed and positioned to exemplify masculine strength, whereas the female body is depicted to emphasize femininity and sexuality. Though most of the published research focuses on female media consumers, male fans are not immune to the negative effects of superhero imagery on how they feel about their bodies. Male superhero fans may have higher levels of self-objectification for two reasons. First, the hypermasculinity that is characteristic of most superhero characters can trigger men to think about themselves in terms of the muscularity and virility of their own bodies. Second, the highly attractive and sexualized women that pepper superhero stories may cause heterosexual men to think about their own appearances, evaluating their own bodies in terms of what kind of masculine appearance might successfully attract such sexually appealing women in the real world.

CONCLUSION

Taken together, the research examining media effects on body image, self-concept, and gender stereotyping demonstrates that even very brief exposure (i.e., 15 minutes or less) to stereotypical images of women in superhero stories can have negative real-world effects on perceptions of the self and on gender stereotyping. Thus, research has consistently demonstrated that entertainment media—even media offerings as fantastical as superhero sagas—are more than "just" entertainment and do impact how we view ourselves and others.

What is particularly interesting about the superhero genre is the potential for both positive and negative effects on gender-related factors. Superhero characters may be empowering, positive influences as well as disempowering, negative influences on gender identity and gender-related beliefs. On the one hand, superheroes may be inspiring and a positive role model for fans. On the other hand, superheroes may promote a narrow view of gender that is problematic when applied to gender-based judgments in the real world.

Media scholars believe it is important that people develop *media literacy* skills as both media consumers and producers. Media literacy skills allow people to understand the constructions of media as well as its potential effects (see the Center for Media Literacy's website for more information on media literacy).[40] Critical awareness of the gender representations present in the stories we love, like superhero sagas, may help us to more meaningfully make sense of these portrayals and understand the workings of the media industry. Further, in the digital age, fans increasingly produce their own superhero stories—in the form of fan fiction, comics, or other art. Media literacy skills can help future superhero writers and producers avoid falling into the trap of producing superhero worlds that narrowly define what it means to be a man or a woman.

NOTES

1. Vorderer, P., & Hartmann, T. (2009). Entertainment and enjoyment as media effects. In J. Bryant and M. B. Oliver (Eds.), *Media effects: Advances in theory and research* (pp. 532–550). New York: Routledge.
2. DeSchepper, B., & Treisman, A. (1996). Visual memory for novel shapes: Implicit coding without attention. *Journal of Experimental Psychology: Learning, Memory, and Cognition, 22,* 27–47.

3. Musen, G., & Treisman, A. (1990). Implicit and explicit memory for visual patterns. *Journal of Experimental Psychology: Learning, Memory, and Cognition, 16,* 127–137.
4. Vorderer & Hartmann (2009).
5. Knight, G. L. (2010). *Female action heroes: A guide to women in comics, video games, film, and television.* Santa Barbara, CA: Greenwood.
6. Calvert, S. L., Kondla, T. A., Ertel, K. A. & Meisel, D. S. (2001). Young adults' perceptions and memories of a televised woman hero. *Sex Roles, 45,* 31–52.
7. Horton, D., & Wohl, R. R. (1956). Mass communication and para-social interaction: Observations on intimacy at a distance. *Psychiatry, 19,* 215–229.
8. Hoffner, C. (1996). Children's wishful identification and parasocial interaction with television characters. *Journal of Broadcasting and Electronic Media, 40,* 389–402.
9. Horton & Wohl (1956).
10. Scott, B. (2010, July 23). Girl geeks are finding their moment in the sun. *USA Today*. Retrieved from EBSCOhost.
11. Hoffner (1996).
12. Cohen, J. (2004). Parasocial break-up from favorite television characters: The role of attachment styles and relationship intensity. *Journal of Social and Personal Relationships, 21,* 187–202; Giles, D. C. (2002). Parasocial interaction: A review of the literature and a model for future research. *Media Psychology, 4,* 279–305.
13. Behm-Morawitz, E., & Mastro, D. (2009). The effects of the sexualization of female video game characters on gender stereotyping and female self-concept. *Sex Roles, 61,* 808–823.
14. Diekman, A., & Murnen, S. K. (2004). Learning to be little women and little men: The inequitable gender equality of nonsexist children's literature. *Sex Roles, 50,* 373–385.
15. Ward, L. M., & Friedman, K. (2006). Using TV as a guide: Associations between television viewing and adolescents' sexual attitudes and behavior. *Journal of Research on Adolescence, 16,* 133–156.

16. Harrison, K. (2000). Television viewing, fat stereotyping, body shape standards, and eating disorder sympomatology in grade school children. *Communication Research, 27,* 617–641.
17. Aubrey, J. S. (2006). Effects of sexually objectifying media on self-objectification and body surveillance in undergraduates: Results of a 2-year panel study. *Journal of Communication, 56,* 366–386.
18. *Editor's Note:* Catwoman's role is sometimes heroic, sometimes villainous, depending on the story.
19. *Editor's Note:* Like Catwoman, Elektra's role is sometimes heroic, sometimes villainous.
20. Knight (2010).
21. Knight (2010).
22. Golombok, S., & Fivush, R. (1994). *Gender development.* New York: Cambridge University Press.
23. Morgan, M. (1987). Television, sex-role attitudes, and sex-role behaviors. *Journal of Early Adolescence, 7,* 269–282.
24. Ward & Friedman (2006).
25. Mulvey, L. (1999). Visual pleasure and narrative cinema. In S. Thornham (Ed.), *Feminist film theory: A reader* (pp. 58–69). New York: New York University Press.
26. Behm-Morawitz & Mastro (2009).
27. Aubrey, J. S., & Harrison, K. (2004). The gender-role content of children's favorite television programs and its links to their gender-related perceptions. *Media Psychology, 6,* 111–146.
    Eisenstock, B. (1984). Sex-role differences in children's identification with counter-stereotypical televised portrayals. *Sex Roles, 10,* 417–430.
28. Lopes, P. D. (2009). *Demanding respect: The evolution of the American comic book.* Philadelphia, PA: Temple University Press.
29. Radway, J. (1984). *Reading the romance: Women, patriarchy, and popular literature.* Chapel Hill: University of North Carolina Press.
30. Festinger, L. (1954). A theory of social comparison processes. *Human Relations, 7,* 117–140.

31. Bessenoff, G. R. (2006). Can the media affect us? Social comparison, self-discrepancy, and the thin ideal. *Psychology of Women Quarterly, 30,* 239–251.
32. Clay, D., Vignoles, V. L., & Dittmar, H. (2005). Body image and self-esteem among adolescent girls: Testing the influence of sociocultural factors. *Journal of Research on Adolescence, 15,* 451–477.
33. Behm-Morawitz & Mastro (2009).
34. Nelson, L. D., & Norton, M. I. (2005). From student to superhero: Situational primes shape future helping. *Journal of Experimental Social Psychology, 41,* 423–430.
35. Taylor, A. (2007). "He's gotta be strong, and he's gotta be fast, and he's gotta be larger than life": Investigating the engendered superhero body. *Journal of Popular Culture, 40,* 344–360.
36. Harrison, K. (2003). Television viewers' ideal body proportions: The case of the curvaceously thin woman. *Sex Roles, 48,* 255–264.
37. Diekman & Murnen (2004); Harrison (2003).
29 Schooler, D., Ward, L. M., Merriwether, A., & Caruthers, A. (2004). Who's that girl: Television's role in the body image development of young White and Black women. *Psychology of Women Quarterly, 28,* 38–47.
38. Agliata, D., & Tantleff-Dunn, S. (2004). The impact of media exposure on males' body image. *Journal of Social and Clinical Psychology, 23,* 7–22. Botta, R. (2003). For your health? The relationship between magazine reading and adolescents' body image and eating disturbances. *Sex Roles, 48,* 389–399.
39. Botta (2003).
32 Fredrickson, B. L., Roberts, T. A., Noll, S. M., Quinn, D. M., & Twenge, J. M. (1998). That swimsuit becomes you: Sex differences in self-objectification, restrained eating, and math performance. *Journal of Personality and Social Psychology, 75,* 269–284.
40. Center for Media Literacy (2002). *Empowerment through education.* Retrieved 2010, from http://www.medialit.org.

PART II

The Humanity of Superheroes

SIX

Our Superheroes, Our Supervillains

Are They All That Different?

Travis Langley

Editor's Note

Each of us has a constellation of personality traits. As you'll discover in this essay by Travis Langley, superheroes and supervillains do too. Langley explains the results of his research on human, superhero, and supervillain personalities. Among the results he shares are how we view the personalities of superheroes in contrast to supervillains, and the ways in which research participants viewed their own personalities as similar to and different from superheroes.

—Robin S. Rosenberg

What distinguishes a superhero from a supervillain? One does good and the other does evil, but what does that mean objectively? Underlying the actions involved in helping or hurting others, in fighting or committing crimes, how do their basic personalities differ?

Can a fictional character have a personality? It's not a person, after all. It's something a person created—in the case of comic book heroes, something a long line of people designed, defined, refined, tweaked, and revised over the course of many stories. If we view personality as someone's characteristic pattern of actions, feelings, and thoughts, while ignoring the fact that a fictional creation isn't technically "someone," then yes, a character has personality. It has a pattern, one that will change between one decade and the next, from one writer to the next, but heaven help the writer whose depiction of that character wanders afar from the pattern readers have accepted. When DC Comics changed grief-stricken Hal Jordan from a valiant Green Lantern into the murderous, megalomaniacal villain Parallax, readers railed that the change was unacceptably "out of character" for such a strong and noble hero. Subsequent attempts to redeem the character fell short. In fact, only by agreeing that yes, it was out of character and by establishing that Parallax was, in fact, not really Hal after all could writer Geoff Johns placate readers, reunite Hal with his green power ring, and save the Green Lantern comic books from their flagging sales.

What specific aspects of personality most specifically define who you are? Whether Iron Man (Tony Stark) prefers pepperoni over anchovy is trivial, not central to understanding his nature, and will not help us predict any strategy he'll follow when wooing women, challenging foes, or wrestling his inner demons. The central concepts invoked most commonly when characterizing comic book heroes and villains largely fall outside psychology's domain. For example, heroes are deemed sane, many villains are not, and heroes who "snap" and turn villainous are said to have gone insane, and yet "insanity" is a legal term, *not* a psychiatric diagnosis. Defined in various ways, it usually means severe mental illness has rendered a defendant (in this case, the villain) unable to distinguish right from wrong and, as defined in some jurisdictions, compelled that person to commit wrongful actions. Although insanity may apply for a defendant experiencing psychosis, which is a broad loss of contact with reality, a person could be psychotic yet sane; even the most bizarre villains generally recognize the rightness and wrongness of their actions, knowing exactly what effect they're having on other human beings in the world around them.

The critical dimension that distinguishes villains from heroes—and the central conflict throughout superhero mythology—is that of good versus evil. Clinicians do not diagnose people as "evil." In and of itself, it's a philosophical and theological subject that involves passing a kind of judgment outside psychology's domain, with some arguing that only actions, not people, are evil.[1] The empirical science of psychology lacks any standard definition for the concept even though some individual psychologists contemplate the nature and origins of evil,[2] considering key properties like selfishness and sadism.[3] Heroes can at times be selfish, even egotistical—taking the law into one's own hands has an inherently narcissistic quality—but the more egotistical they are, they less heroic we perceive them to be and the more prepared we are to see them go bad. Batman is more heroic than the Punisher[4] not only because he will not kill, but because his motives are less selfish. Whereas the Punisher wages his vigilante war out of anger, Batman controls his anger and fights the good fight for the sake of the potential victims, to keep others from suffering the tragedy that struck his family. An antihero like the Punisher is more selfish than the hero, and the villain is more selfish than either one, but real villainy requires something more. Galactus, among the most powerful, most destructive beings, in all of comics, is amoral, not immoral, when he devours planets, sometimes killing billions of lesser life forms. He takes no delight in it. He simply feeds. In some versions, Superman's archnemesis Lex Luthor, on the contrary, gets his "kicks" by causing the deaths of innocent people (*Superman: The Movie*).

These broad dimensions of sanity versus insanity and good versus evil, while critical in distinguishing comic book heroes and villains as depicted in the comics, merely describe behavior instead of explaining it, and they do not present complexity of character. A Hal Jordan who wields a bow and arrow instead of his Green Lantern ring, while probably just as sane and good as comic book archers like his friend Green Arrow or Marvel Comics' Hawkeye, would not be identical in personality to either one. There are many other dimensions to who we are. What's left for the mental health professional who wants to step beyond mental illness or goodness when exploring character complexity?

Some of those other dimensions are *personality factors*—clusters of cognitive, emotional, and behavioral personality traits that tend to go together. A person who is outgoing, energetic, and assertive is also likely to be sociable, impulsive, and fearless, so we'd call that person *extraverted*. No single trait pegs the person as extraverted, and the extravert can still have some introverted qualities, but an overall tendency to show more extraverted than introverted characteristics leads to that assessment. Researchers have identified various personality factors like dominance[5] and psychoticism.[6] Cattell identified 16 personality factors, whereas Eysenck proposed a three-factor theory, but numerous other researchers have found that personality traits cluster into five global factors commonly called the *Big Five*—five factors that sum up a great portion of an individual's personality, are statistically distinct from each other, and show universality in that we can identify these factors in virtually any group of people.[7] While researchers disagree on how to interpret these Big Five factors, differing on what they mean, on which aspects are most important, and even on what to name them all, a surprising degree of consistency across many empirical investigations has emerged in measuring these five, known by some as the OCEAN model[8]: openness, conscientiousness, extraversion, agreeableness, neuroticism.

THE ERIICA PROJECT

My students and I investigate issues related to personality and behavior as part of our ongoing ERIICA Project (Empirical Research on the Interpretation and Influence of the Comic Arts). We have collected information from nearly two thousand college students, online survey respondents, prison inmates, fan convention attendees, and more, who rate themselves and others on characteristics including optimism, self-esteem, and the Big Five factors. We always ask respondents to rate themselves first because doing so helps them understand the factors better before they rate other people and fictional characters on those same factors. We correlate how they see themselves with how they see whomever else we ask them to rate, which varies from one set of data we collect to another. Participants variously rate the personalities of their favorite superhero, most superheroes, their favorite supervillain, most supervillains, and others. As of this writing, 1,017 participants have rated themselves, fictional characters, and others on the OCEAN factors in response to different surveys.[9] In what follows, I compare our participants' ratings of superheroes, supervillains, and themselves, and discuss what these differences might mean (Table 6.1).

Openness

In 1961's *Fantastic Four* #1, scientist Reed Richards builds his own spaceship, takes his three closest friends along as the crew for its first experimental journey, and accidentally gets them all exposed to cosmic rays that mutate them. After their crash landing, they emerge from the spaceship with superpowers that reflect their respective personalities: Intellectually flexible Richards become the stretchable Mr. Fantastic; tough Ben Grimm becomes the strong, rock-skinned Thing; hot-headed Johnny Storm, the Human Torch; and originally reticent Sue Storm, the Invisible Girl.

Why did Richards build that rocket? Openness refers to being open to new experiences. People high in this personality factor are inquisitive, creative, and analytical, willing to try things that are unfamiliar, nontraditional, and new. Their thinking is

Table 6.1. *OCEAN Ratings*. 1,017 respondents rated themselves on the factors of the OCEAN model across four sets of collected data. 420 of them also rated superheroes. 303 of them rated supervillains. All scores are on 0–100 scales.

	Self	**Favorite Superhero**	**Most Superheroes**	**Favorite Supervillain**	**Most Supervillains**
Openness	79.28	69.73	69.88	63.78	56.36
Conscientiousness	69.65	75.22	79.32	59.37	56.12
Extraversion	66.09	64.24	73.23	53.51	53.58
Agreeableness	73.29	66.71	73.83	25.70	27.06
Neuroticism	40.24	41.78	40.08	63.51	65.31

divergent, unconventional, and independent. Their curiosity knows no bounds. Upon hearing a riddle, those high in openness do not want you to tell them the answer. For them, the fun lies in figuring it out. They can enjoy adventure for the sake of trying something interesting and new—but not necessarily out of any need for thrills and excitement. Building his own spaceship and rocketing off with the three people closest to him for the sheer challenge of it, Reed Richards exemplifies this factor.

People low in openness distrust novelty, eschew the unfamiliar, and stick with the tried and true. Their actions will include traditional ways of doing things, conventional behavior, and adherence to simple, unsubtle solutions. They distrust originality and intellectualism, and disparage the value of art. Please note, though, that a person high in many traits that are part of openness may be low in other traits that are also part of openness. For example, even though openness is often intellectual in nature,[10] specific individuals can be open to new experience without including the intellectual aspects, as illustrated by Kenny and Kenny's study[11] in which psychological professionals who assessed characters from *The Simpsons* on OCEAN factors considered Homer and Bart Simpson—no scholars there—to be the most open. Neither character would welcome an academic challenge, but both will go to creative, even convoluted lengths to get the things they want, as when Bart plays elaborate pranks. They leap into a wide variety of endeavors and experiences.

ERIICA Project respondents who completed our OCEAN inventories viewed themselves as highly open to experience, more so than superheroes. They considered their respective favorite supervillains even lower in openness and yet higher than average for supervillains. How can we understand this result? Perhaps readers carry biases that predispose them to perceive greater complexity in individuals they like and groups with whom they identify.[12] In fact, greater familiarity with any group creates more opportunities to recognize variety across the group and within each of its members[13]—in this case, reading about heroes more than villains and favorite characters more than least favorite characters.

Conscientiousness

Historically, the Riddler's obsession with puzzles and his compulsion to send Batman clue-bearing riddles impeded his criminal success. Would the Riddler be considered high on the personality factor of conscientiousness? Conscientious individuals plan, persist, organize, set higher goals, and follow tasks through to completion;[14] no surprise then that conscientiousness predicts successful job performance best out of the Big Five.[15] However, taking any of these conscientious characteristics to the extremes can be counterproductive. A perfectionist can be overconscientious, demonstrating inflexibility, perfectionism, unrealistic expectations, and a preoccupation for details that can blind that person to greater priorities and interfere with meeting the very goals the person feels so driven to fulfill.

ERIICA participants rated superheroes as more conscientious than themselves, and themselves more conscientious than the villains, so they appear to see a positive correlation between conscientiousness and heroism—conversely, a negative correlation between conscientiousness and villainy—even though many villains show elaborate attention to detail, drive to succeed at any cost, and conscientious devotion to their goals. This may mean that participants want to believe that good is more conscientious than evil, or maybe they consider effectiveness integral to conscientiousness. Batman's success in foiling the Riddler's meticulous plans may make him seem more conscientious overall, even in areas where conscientiousness does not really predict achievement.

Extraversion

"Outgoing" is the most common descriptor for an extravert. The extravert is likely to be active, talkative, socially aware, and outwardly focused, more attentive to his or her environment than their own inner workings, as opposed to the shy, nervous, inwardly focused introvert. In general, extraverts also tend to be more fearless,[16] thereby sharing greater capacity for both heroic and criminal behavior.[17] After conscientiousness, extraversion best predicts occupational success. Extraverts may be outwardly friendly, but not necessarily so. A person's outgoing actions can be pushy, provocative, or otherwise obnoxious. Extraverts can also be impulsive, seek excitement, and lack inhibitions, which raises the odds that they will break the law. Extraverts who commit crimes more frequently use dramatic, powerful firearms, whereas introverts gravitate toward quieter instruments like cutlery.[18] Most costumed vigilantes, like the villains they fight, are breaking the law. They trespass, stalk, carry unlicensed weapons, and come crashing through windows all the time.

In fact, of all five factors, extraversion correlates most strongly with lawbreaking actions. As Bartol and Bartol put it, "Because extraverts have higher needs for excitement and stimulation to break the daily boredom, they are also most likely to run counter to the law."[19] While this relationship may relate to the aforementioned fearlessness, it may instead result from other tendencies more consistently found among extraverts like *sensation seeking*, "the need for varied, novel, and complex sensations and experiences, and the willingness to take physical and social risks for the sake of such experiences."[20]

Despite the real-world relationship between extraversion and criminal behavior, ERIICA respondents expected most superheroes to be highly extraverted with many outgoing qualities and supervillains to fall right in the middle of the extraversion-introversion dimension. Heroes must be brave and socially bold. Participants saw themselves and their favorite superheroes, as predicted, close to each other somewhere between supervillains and the rest of the superheroes. Conscious of our own inner experience, we recognize that we're not always as outgoing as we'd like to be even if we like to see ourselves as being more sociable than villains. However much we want our heroes to be brave and socially bold, our favorite heroes sometimes need a dose of inner conflict and turmoil lest their confidence come across as sheer arrogance.

One complicating issue in this assessment may be the fact that individuals often confuse *antisocial* with *unsociable*. An antisocial individual, behaving antithetically to society's rules and norms through actions like breaking laws or otherwise violating the rights of others, may be variously socially outgoing or reserved. It's a separate issue. In addition, whether a person is extraverted or introverted is a separate issue from how likable that person is. Whereas one outgoing person may be very friendly, another can be utterly obnoxious—that is, disagreeable.

Agreeableness

Agreeableness does not mean a person will simply agree to anything, although many agreeable persons are so inclined. It's an older use of the word, meaning friendly, good-natured, easy to get along with—"he's an agreeable fellow." Complete agreeableness can be a problem because those who place getting along with others above all their other priorities may have trouble asserting themselves or fighting for what's right. ERIICA respondents rated themselves and superheroes as being very agreeable, considering themselves to be just as agreeable as most superheroes. Evidently, though, they want their heroes to be even more likable, rating heroes as being more agreeable than superheroes or themselves. In contrast, it comes as no surprise that they rated supervillains very low in this factor.

Neuroticism

"Neurosis" is not a modern diagnostic term for many reasons, not the least of which is that the majority of professionals disagree with Sigmund Freud's thinking that underlies the concept; nonetheless the adjective "neurotic" has endured. Peter Parker gets treated as the poster child for "neurotic" superheroes: an uncertain, imperfect bundle of worries. Unlike Superman's nebbishy Clark Kent act, Peter Parker does not have to put on a neurotic act. In his role as Spider-Man, Parker uses humor heavily as a defense mechanism, which helps him both to hide extensive insecurities from enemies and to shove those insecurities from the forefront of his thoughts.

Neuroticism, emotional instability, is an enduring tendency to experience negative emotional states. Individuals high in neuroticism are more prone to feeling tense, rattled, guilty, or angry, and to suffer more anxiety and depression than others.[21] Responding more poorly to environmental stress, they may interpret everyday difficulties as catastrophes, and feel hopeless over minor frustrations. If introverted, they're likely to be self-conscious and shy, as opposed to introverts low on neuroticism, who more contentedly enjoy focusing on their own inner experience. In fact, individuals low in neuroticism and therefore high in emotional stability stay calmer under pressure, worry less, and maintain a more even keel. Emotionally stable individuals experience less of the negative emotionality associated with neuroticism, although not necessarily the positive emotions more strongly associated with extraversion.[22]

ERIICA respondents saw supervillains as being high in neuroticism while clumping themselves and superheroes together on the more emotionally stable end of the neuroticism dimension. Although emotionally stable individuals wield greater coping skills with lower rates of anxiety and mood disorders,[23] having too little emotional reactivity can pose problems as well. Perfect emotional stability would mean that emotions fluctuate too little, and so the person may seem insensitive and without feelings. Emotions need to vary in nature and intensity. Moods should change. In some situations, feeling terrible is the most appropriate, most normal, thing. *Star Trek*'s Vulcans strive for such stability but we see it as inhuman. The Vision, an android superhero in the Avengers, typically eschews emotion, even though comic book writer Roy Thomas quickly established that even an android can cry, exposing his emotions to readers.

BEYOND THE BIG FIVE

Other personality factors like leadership combine elements of the Big Five. Strong leaders tend to be extraverted, conscientious, and emotionally stable.[24] Agreeableness does not correlate with leadership in a straightforward manner because the desire to be likable can impede assertiveness. Outgoing optimists like Superman and Captain America make good leaders because they inspire others and fill them with hope. Batman is arguably the best strategist among the superheroes, but this hero with no superpowers tends to unnerve the others. He works better when teaming up with individual heroes. When leading a team like the Outsiders, he manages for a while but eventually and invariably drives them away. Effective leadership requires a good fit between leadership style, the followers' needs, and the demands of the situation.

What about leaders of supercriminal organizations? Such organizations tend to fall apart more readily than do superhero teams, not only because superheroes break up those organizations but also because the supervillains' criminal nature is, almost by definition, largely selfish, untrustworthy, and disloyal. Villainous leaders tend to butt heads with each other. Whereas superheroes who disagree may be motivated to work things out for the greater good, each supercriminal's first concern is usually self-interest, and they may have difficulty taking others' points of view. Criminal leaders, while better than those they lead when it comes to seeing the bigger picture, are nevertheless ready to stab an associate in the back. Heroes don't take charge by killing their rivals.

GOOD GUYS OR BAD GUYS?

How are superheroes and supervillains most alike? Our ERIICA Project respondents rated the heroes as more open, conscientious, extraverted, and agreeable (vastly more agreeable) and less neurotic than the villains, and saw themselves as being more like the heroes on every dimension. No dimension emerged in which respondents expected heroes' personalities in general to match those of the villains. On the one hand, our findings show that readers distinguish heroes and villains more elaborately than simply categorizing them as good or evil, sane or insane. On the other hand, expecting them to differ in all dimensions may suggest excessive readiness to dichotomize them, reluctance to acknowledge where heroes and villains might be similar, unrealistic ideals for heroes to live up to, or naive beliefs that only monsters perform monstrous deeds. People often underestimate how abominably normal, healthy people can behave and overestimate how well overt behaviors, especially evil actions, reflect their performers' ingrained personalities.[25]

Fans' ratings of criminals differ greatly from empirical findings on the relationship between extraversion and criminal behavior in the real world. If fans have misjudged the characters on that dimension, might they have rated other dimensions poorly as well? Perhaps they rated characters appropriately but the characters' creators failed to depict realistic criminals. Then again, supercriminals likely differ from real world criminals in the first place. Psychologists with extensive knowledge of the characters' histories and behavior might assess the characters more accurately, but then again, an "accurate" assessment may be irrelevant when we're looking at the relationship between how fans view their superheroes and themselves.

Despite some perceptions of criminals as "a superstitious, cowardly lot," as Bruce Wayne famously put it in Batman's origin (*Detective Comics* #33, 1940), one similarity between heroes and criminals can be the fearlessness associated with some aspects of extraversion or at least the ability to overcome great fear.[26] Adventurers and psychopaths seek excitement through a variety of means. Ultimately the greatest similarity between superheroes and supervillains—in terms of personalities, not powers—may be the flamboyance that sets them apart from real world heroes and evildoers. These characters do not simply fight or commit crime. Most fight or commit crime while wearing costumes.

NOTES

1. Horne, M. (2008). Evil acts, not evil people: Their characteristics and contents. *Journal of Analytical Psychology*, *53*, 669–690.
2. Staub, E. (1989). *The roots of evil: The origins of genocide and other group violence.* New York; Cambridge University Press.

   Waller, J. (2002). *Becoming evil: How ordinary people commit genocide and mass killing.* New York: Oxford University Press.

3. Stone, M. H. (2010). Sexual sadism: A portrait of evil. *Journal of the American Academy of Psychoanalysis and Dynamic Psychiatry*, *38*, 133–157.

4. *Editor's Note:* The Punisher (aka Frank Castle) is a Marvel character; Frank's wife and children happened to witness the mob murder people and then they themselves were killed by the mob. Castle devoted the rest of this life to get the mob and other criminals by any means necessary, including murder.

5. Cattell, H. E. P, & Mead, A. D. (2008). The sixteen personality factor questionnaire (16PF). In G. Boyle, G. Matthews, & D. H. Saklofske (Eds.), *The Sage handbook of personality theory and assessment, Vol. 2. Personality measurement and testing* (pp. 135–178). Los Angeles, CA: Sage.
6. Eysenck, H. J. (1990). Genetic and environmental contributions to individual differences: The three major dimensions of personality. *Journal of Personality*, *58*, 245–261.
7. Fiske, D. W. (1949). Consistency of the factorial structures of personality ratings from different sources. *Journal of Abnormal Social Psychology*, *44*, 329–344.
   McCrae, R. R., & Costa, P. T., Jr. (1987). Validation of the five-factor model across instruments and observers. *Journal of Personality and Social Psychology*, *52*, 81–90.
   Digman, J. M. (1990). Personality structure: Emergence of the five-factor model. *Annual Review of Psychology*, *41*, 417–440.
8. John, O. P. (1990). The "Big Five" factor taxonomy: Dimensions of personality in the natural language and in questionnaires. In L. A. Pervin (Ed.), *Handbook of personality: Theory and research* (pp. 66–100). New York: Guilford.
9. Cate, C. L, Langley, N., Poole , J, & Langley, T. (2008, April). *Home is where the Hulk is: Comic book convention bolsters fans' self esteem*. Presented at the annual meeting of the Arkansas Academy of Science. Arkadelphia, Arkansas.
   Langley, T., & Duncan, R. (2008, February). *How heavy is that cape? Challenges in empirical assessment of comics' influence and fans' behavior*.

Symposium presented at the Comics Arts Conference, WonderCon. San Francisco, California.

10. Arteche, A., Chamorro-Premuzic, T., Ackerman, P., & Furnham, A. (2009). Typical intellectual engagement as a byproduct of openness, learning approaches, and self-assessed intelligence. *Educational Psychology*, *29*, 357–367.
11. Kenny, D. A., & Kenny, D. T. (2006). The personalities of The Simpsons. In A. Brown (Ed.), *D'oh! The psychology of the Simpsons* (pp. 187–200). Dallas: BenBella Books.
12. Allen, V. L., & Wilder, D. A. (1979). Group categorization and attribution of belief similarity. *Small Group Behavior*, *10*, 73–80.
    Park, B., & Rothbart, M. (1982). Perception of out-group homogeneity and levels of social categorization: Memory for the subordinate attributes of in-group and out-group members. *Journal of Personality and Social Psychology*, *42*, 1051–1068.
13. Linville, P. W., Gischer, G. W., & Salovey, P. (1989). Perceived distributions of the characteristics of in-group and out-group members. Empirical evidence and a computer simulation. *Journal of Personality and Social Psychology*, *15*, 509–522.
14. Judge, T. A., Higgins, C. A., Thoresen, C. J., & Barrick, M. R. (1999). The Big Five personality traits, general mental ability, and career success across the life span. *Personnel Psychology*, *52*, 621–652.
    Poropat, A. E. (2009). A meta-analysis of the Five-Factor Model of personality and academic performance. *Psychological Bulletin*, *135*, 322–338.
15. Barrick, M. R., Mount, M. K., & Judge, T. A. (2001). Personality and performance at the beginning of the new millennium: What do we know and where to go next? *International Journal of Selection and Assessment*, *91*, 9–30.
    Hurtz, G. M., & Donovan, J. J. (2000). Personality and job performance: The Big Five revisited. *Journal of Applied Psychology*, *85*, 869–879.
    Salgado, J. R. (1997). The five factor model of personality and job performance in the European Community. *Journal of Applied Psychology*, *82*, 30–43.

16. Gilbert, A. M., Gilbert, B. O., & Gilbert, D. G. (1994). Fears as a function of gender and extraversion in adolescents. *Journal of Social Behavior and Personality*, *9*, 89–94.
Pineles, S. L., Vogt, D. S., & Orr, S. P. (2009). Personality and fear responses during conditioning: Beyond extraversion. *Personality and Individual Differences, 46,* 48–53.
17. Numerous—but not all—researchers find extraversion to correlate with fearlessness. Pineles, Vogt, and Orr (2009) note that these equivocal findings appear to depend on which aspects of extraversion the various investigators measure.
18. Labato, A. (2000). Criminal weapon use in Brazil: A psychological analysis. In D. Canter & L. Alison (Eds.), *Profiling property crimes* (Vol. 4, pp. 107–145). Dartmouth, UK: Ashgate.
19. Bartol, C. R., & Bartol, A. M. (2010). Criminal behavior: A psychosocial approach (10th ed.). Upper Saddle River, NJ: Pearson, p. 102.
20. Zuckerman, M. (1979). *Sensation seeking: Beyond the optimum level of arousal*. Hillsdale, NJ: Erlbaum, p. 27.
21. Matthews, G., & Deary, I. J. (1998). *Personality traits*. Cambridge, UK: Cambridge University Press.
22. Myers, D. (1992). *The pursuit of happiness: Who is happy—and why*. New York: Morrow.
23. Bouchard, G. (2003). Cognitive appraisals, neuroticism, and openness as correlates of coping strategies: An integrative model of adaptation to marital difficulties. *Journal of Behavioural Science/Revue canadienne des sciences due comportement*, *35*, 1–12.
Brown, T. A., & Rosellini, A. J. (2011). The direct and indirect effects of neuroticism and life stress on the severity and longitudinal course of depressive symptoms. *Journal of Abnormal Psychology*, *120*, 844–856.
Wang, S., Repetti, R. L., & Campos, B. (2011). Job stress and family social behavior: The moderating role of neuroticism. *Journal of Occupational Health Psychology*, *16*, 441–456.
24. Hirschfeld, R. R., Jordan, M. H., Thomas, C. H., & Feild, H. S. (2008). Observed leadership potential of personnel in a team setting: Big

five traits and proximal factors as predictors. *International Journal of Selection and Assessment*, *16*, 385–402.

25. Zimbardo, P. (2008). *The Lucifer effect*. New York: Random House.
26. Langley, T. (2012). *Batman and psychology: A dark and stormy knight*. New York: Wiley.

SEVEN

Are Superheroes Just SuperGifted?

Robin S. Rosenberg and Ellen Winner

EDITOR'S NOTE

Superhero stories are ultimately about people who are gifted—who have abilities that are significantly better than most people. Even human superheroes are gifted. Robin S. Rosenberg and Ellen Winner combine their expertise about the psychology of superheroes and the psychology of being gifted to discover whether the giftedness of human superheroes like Bruce Wayne and Tony Stark follows the same path as that of people who are gifted in our world.

—Robin S. Rosenberg

As psychologists, when we read or watch superhero stories, we are struck by the ways that superheroes are *gifted* people. Some of the issues they struggle with—discovering that they are different from other people, learning to use and harness their gifts, figuring out their place in the world—are the issues that gifted people face as well. How far does the similarity go? Are the superheroes in fiction our gifted children in reality? In this essay we consider what is known about gifted children and draw comparisons between such children and superheroes. In many cases, the comparisons are very close.

Like superheroes, gifted children display abilities out of step with their peers. They show advanced levels in one or more areas at ages far younger than shown by typical children. Intellectually gifted children, for instance, may begin to read fluently at the age of three or four, without any extended instruction; they may play a musical instrument as skillfully as a highly trained adult; they may turn everyday experiences into mathematical problems to play with, moving from arithmetic to algebra before their peers have learned to carry numbers in addition.[1] Some gifted children show precocious abilities in nonacademic domains including drawing, dance, mimicry and role-play, chess, and athletics.

Superheroes are clearly much like gifted children. They are *super*heroes because of their extraordinary talents and abilities. Some superheroes were born that way—with powers and abilities so far beyond those of mortals that they are not human and never were; they were born super*gifted*. Aquaman, Wonder Woman, each of the Incredibles, and Hellboy are examples. Other superheroes aren't fully human, yet weren't born manifesting "gifts"; rather, they developed their gifts during childhood or adolescence. Examples of this group include various X-Men, such as Phoenix (Jean Grey, who manifested telepathy) and Pyro (Saint-John Allerdyce, whose gift is the ability to manipulate fire).

Still other superheroes were born fully human, but even as children were intellectually gifted—they were much "smarter" at academic subjects than were their peers. Bruce Wayne (Batman), Tony Stark (Iron Man), and Peter Parker (Spider-Man) are examples; their intellectual gifts were obvious during their childhoods. Wayne dedicated himself to the basic sciences necessary for a forensic career, and Stark learned about physics and various types of engineering. Parker, too, devoted himself to scientific studies.

All the superheroes mentioned above were, in one way or another, gifted children or adolescents. And gifted children, it turns out, tend to have in common certain features and experiences; the stories of superheroes who were gifted as youngsters often reflect these findings.

THE JAGGED COGNITIVE PROFILES OF GIFTED CHILDREN AND SUPERHEROES

Psychologists typically assess academic giftedness with an IQ test that yields subtest scores as well as an overall, global number.

Children are usually defined as gifted if their global IQ score rises above some arbitrary cutoff point (often 130, where the average score is 100). The assumption underlying the use of a global score is that academically gifted children are generally gifted in all academic subjects. Some children justify this assumption perfectly by demonstrating giftedness in reading, math, and logical analytic thinking. These kinds of children are *notationally gifted*, able to master rapidly the two kinds of notational symbol systems valued in school: language and numbers. Globally gifted children can be thought of as analogous to Superboy or Superman: possessing many, and varied, high abilities, and thus standing out among even gifted people, just as Superman, but virtue of his multiple powers and abilities, stands out among superheroes.

Although globally gifted children certainly exist, many other academically gifted children present a much less balanced picture; unevenness between verbal and mathematical abilities may be the rule, not the exception. Academically gifted children often reveal jagged profiles, and a gift in one scholastic area does not imply a gift in another area. For example, one study[2] found that the higher the IQ, the more variability among the subtests that make up the IQ test. Thus, it is more common to find mathematical ability far higher than verbal ability in a high-IQ individual than in a low-IQ individual.

IQ subtests fall into two groups to yield a *verbal* IQ and a *performance* IQ. Whereas verbal tests require skills that rely on language (such as understanding and explaining what certain words mean), performance subtests rely much less on language, if at all, and require skills related to perceiving and manipulating objects and numbers. Children who have a high IQ can have a significant discrepancy between their verbal and performance IQ scores,[3] and the same goes for high scorers on the SAT test—almost half of students scoring in the top 0.5 percent on the SATs had math and verbal SAT scores that were different by more than 100 points (over one standard deviation apart). In contrast, almost three-quarters of students scoring in the very top—0.01—had such a differentiated profile.[4]

It is not surprising that such unevenness exists, because the abilities that underlie mathematical giftedness differ sharply from those that underlie verbal giftedness, just as the abilities that underlie physical superstrength are different from the abilities that underlie X-ray vision or telepathy. As just one example, spatial abilities underlie mathematical but not verbal giftedness.[5]

Jagged profiles also characterize children gifted in music and art. A gift in music or art can exist alongside an average or even a lower-than-average IQ. In fact, if you've got intelligence that is at least average, your IQ won't predict your musical ability. Yet musically gifted children typically do very well academically.[6] One possible explanation for this conflicting set of findings is that all our knowledge of the relation between music, IQ, and academic skills comes from studies of children taking classical music lessons. These children are likely to come from educated parents who provide enriched family environments.

Children gifted in the visual arts and in athletics typically show a lack of interest in academic achievement, as was true of Oliver Queen (who became the Green Arrow), who was a gifted archer but a poor academic student. People gifted in the visual arts are even less committed academically than those in athletics.[7]

A word about intellectually gifted children: they tend to score high on moral reasoning tests. That is, the have a precocious understanding of morality, well beyond their years. They ask moral questions—about right and wrong, about whether it is better to take a life if it saves more lives later—that their same-age nongifted peers won't think about for years. But thinking about questions of morality isn't the same as behaving morally, and intellectually gifted children don't behave any more morally than do their nongifted peers. Thus, the rigid superhero moral code cannot be explained as an outgrowth of the superhero's intellectual gifts. Rather, it must stem from their values and those of the culture in which they work. (Of course some antiheroes, such as the Punisher and the Sub-Mariner, do not adhere to this code, which is what distinguishes them as antiheroes rather than superheroes.)

ARE GIFTED CHILDREN AND SUPERHEROES BORN OR MADE?

As we noted earlier, some superheroes were born super (e.g., Wonder Woman, the *Incredibles* family members); their giftedness emerged at birth, dubbed the "nature" explanation for giftedness. In contrast, other superheroes, such as Batman and Green Arrow, had to train hard to become superheroes, dubbed the "nurture" explanation for giftedness. Which model of acquiring giftedness is the more accurate reflection of what we know about human giftedness?

Nurture: Giftedness Is Made

Some psychologists argue that giftedness (in any domain) is entirely a product of what is referred to as goal-directed hard work, or *deliberate practice*. For instance, in one study researchers showed that levels of expertise in piano, violin, chess, bridge, and athletics correlate directly with the amount of deliberate practice.[8] Researchers in this camp argue that there is no systematic and verifiable evidence for high abilities emerging prior to extensive periods of deliberate practice. They discount as unreliable anecdotal reports about the childhood feats of prodigies such as Mozart, Gauss, and Menuhin, who can be seen as the real-life equivalent of Wonder Woman or Aquaman: born gifted.

Consistent with this contemporary nurture view of giftedness are several other earlier findings. First, case studies of creative people show that all great achievement is associated with years of deep and prolonged work.[9] For example, it took Newton 20 years to go from his preliminary ideas to his magnum opus, *Principia Mathematica*.[10]

Another research result may or may not surprise fans of Batman and Iron Man: Outstanding achievement in science was predicted by the participants' capacity for endurance, concentration, and commitment rather than their level of intellectual ability.[11] (However, the scientists who participated in this study were all high in intellectual ability to begin with.) Anne Roe's studies thus show that high ability is not sufficient for exceptional achievement; rather, one needs both high ability and perseverance in order to harness, channel, and enhance ability. In fact, Benjamin Bloom showed that eminent adults in a variety of domains did not achieve high levels of performance without a long and intensive period of training.[12] Their training began in early childhood with warm and loving teachers, who were then supplanted by more demanding and rigorous master teachers.

Nature: Giftedness Is Innate—At Least Somewhat

Bloom's study might be taken as evidence that the high levels of achievement attained were entirely the result of the rigorous training. However, a careful look at the descriptions of these eminent individuals as children shows that at a very young age, prior to any regimen of training or deliberate practice, signs of unusual ability were present. The musicians were described as quick to learn the piano, and both their parents and their teachers recognized they were special. The sculptors said that they drew constantly as children, usually realistically. The mathematicians recalled being obsessed with gears, valves, gauges, and dials and were considered "brilliant" as children.

The problem for researchers is how to sort out the various factors: Children who have the most ability are also likely to be those who are most interested in a particular activity, who begin to work at that activity at an early age, and who work the hardest at it. Ericsson's research demonstrated the importance of hard work but did not rule out the role of innate ability.

Although Ericsson and his colleagues consider the stories of early (pretraining) achievements of child prodigies to be unreliable,[13] there are simply too many such reports that are too consistent with one another for them to be easily discounted. In addition, these reports come not only from potentially biased parents but also from careful case studies of young prodigies.[14] If exceptional abilities emerge prior to intensive instruction and training, then these abilities are likely to reflect atypical, innate potential. So we can answer the question of whether hard work is all that is needed for someone to become gifted. The answer is that whereas intensive training is necessary for the acquisition of *expertise*; it does not sufficiently explain children's high level of achievement.[15]

How does all this fit with how superheroes are depicted?

Some "fully human" superheroes, such as Batman and Iron Man are gifted with significantly above average intelligence, but they honed their abilities through intensive and persistent practice, Ericsson's *deliberate practice*. As a child, young Bruce Wayne witnessed his parents' senseless murder and vowed to avenge their deaths by dedicating the rest of his life "warring on all criminals" (*Detective Comics #33*, 1939). This he did by systematically learning what he needed to learn, and then practicing it until he fully mastered the body of knowledge—whether it was chemical reactions or flying sidekicks. Similarly, as a child, genius inventor Tony Stark was creating advanced technological devices and solving engineering problems well beyond his years (and he entered college at Massachusetts Institute of Technology at the age of 15, graduating four years later with a bachelor's degree *and two masters degrees*). He accomplished these feats through intensive mastery of the relevant content areas and applying that knowledge. In the nonacademic realm, the fully human Oliver Queen, who later becomes Green Arrow, discovered as a child that he had a fantastic aptitude for archery; Queen said that after famed archer Howard Hill gave young Queen archery lessons, Hill exclaimed that Queen was "the best he'd ever seen" at archery.[16] Queen may have had an aptitude, but his amazing archery skills were honed by concerted effort and practice. This is also true of Batman and Iron Man; their "talents" alone would not have gotten them as far if they hadn't diligently worked at their crafts.

But like gifted children, our superheroes must have been born with an innate predisposition to learn rapidly in a particular domain. If not, how could they be motivated to work so hard to improve their skills? Oliver Queen worked at improving his archery skills, in part, because he showed an aptitude for it, which led him to enjoy the challenge of improving his skills, which in turn motivated him to spend more hours at practice. (The other reason he practiced his skills, according to the origin story in *Green Arrow: Year One*, is that those skills helped him survive after he was marooned on an island.) Similarly, as a child, Tony Stark enjoyed learning about various types of engineering and other sciences, and so his form of "play" was to immerse himself in inventing, learning with each creation.

It is useful to consider the contrast between gifted children and autistic savants. Gifted children clearly are born with an unusual capacity to develop a skill in some domain, and the evidence for this is the early age at which their exceptional skill emerges. But these children often take years to develop their skills to adult level. In contrast, some autistic savants seem to demonstrate full-blown high levels of skills right from the start, without even practicing. We have accounts of savants picking out tunes on the piano the first time they ever touched the keys, or drawing highly realistic drawings almost as soon as they begin to draw. Perhaps gifted children are more like fully human superheroes (such as Batman, Iron Man, and Green Arrow), whereas autistic savants are more like *super*human superheroes who were born with full-blown superhuman abilities (such as Wonder Woman and Aquaman). Consider that, like humans who learn to harness their gifts later in life, Superman had to learn to control his powers so that he didn't hurt people when he pulled them from a burning building. However, the type of practice needed to control superpowers is depicted as less than what we know is needed for a human to develop skills and abilities to the "super" level—making them all the more superhuman.

ARE THE FAMILIES OF SUPERHEROES LIKE THOSE OF GIFTED CHILDREN?

The notion that giftedness is a product of intensive training reflects an overly optimistic view of the power of nurture. A more negative view of the power of nurture is reflected in another common claim: that gifted children are created by driving, overambitious parents. There is concern that the end result of such extreme pushing will be disengagement, bitterness, and depression. Parents of gifted children are advised to let their children have a normal childhood. However, most gifted children do not become bitter and disaffected. Moreover, although Bruce Wayne was driven (by himself, not directly by his parents or guardian) into becoming a superhero through near-constant practice, in our world it is impossible to drive an ordinary child to the kinds of high achievements seen in gifted children. Parental prodding can't cause of giftedness.

That's not to say that parents don't have an important role. In fact, gifted children typically report that their family played a positive, not a negative, role in their development.[17] The families of gifted children are child centered, meaning that family life is often totally focused on the child's needs.[18] However, the fact that parents spend a great deal of time with their gifted children does not mean that they create the gift. It is likely that parents first notice signs of exceptionality and then respond by devoting themselves to the development of their child's extraordinary ability. Of course, we have no information on the number of child-centered families that do not produce gifted children (which would serve as a control-group).

Gifted children typically grow up in enriched family environments with a high level of intellectual or artistic stimulation.[19] Of course, these findings are correlational. We cannot conclude that stimulation and enrichment lead to the development of giftedness. Gifted children may need an unusual amount of stimulation and may demand enriched environments, a demand to which their parents respond. Thus, the child's inborn ability could be the driving force, leading the child to select enriched environments.[20] Again, we don't know how many children of enriched environments display no signs of giftedness.

Parents of gifted children typically both have high expectations and model hard work and high achievement themselves.[21] It is logically possible that gifted children have simply inherited their gift from their parents, who also happen to be hardworking achievers. This appears to have been true of Tony Stark, whose father, Howard Stark, was a successful engineer and inventor. As a child Tony, like many gifted children, found "work" to be his play—he enjoyed tinkering and so his perseverance and practice would have felt no different than a youngster persevering at and practicing a computer game in order to get to the next level or win the game.

While we know that the families of gifted children (at least of those in our society) tend to have these positive characteristics, we cannot conclude that particular family characteristics play a role in causing the development of giftedness—for two reasons. First, studies don't have relevant control groups. Second, if family characteristics contribute to giftedness, we still can't say whether aspects of parenting contribute to giftedness, or whether something about the (gifted) child elicits certain behaviors from other family members.

What of about the families of superheroes? Typically, human superheroes were orphaned during their childhoods, as were Bruce Wayne, Oliver Queen, and Peter Parker. There is some evidence that the childhoods of creative geniuses were rife with trauma including early parental death.[22] Our stories of human superheroes seem to reflect this pattern.

There is a way in which the orphaned gifted youngsters who became superheroes share a characteristic typical of gifted children in our world: lots of independence during childhood. Parents of gifted children grant their children more than the usual amount of independence.[23] Bruce Wayne had a lot of independence while growing up (some might say too much) to pursue his passions. Peter Parker, while tied to family obligations more than were Wayne and Stark, was allowed and encouraged to pursue his passion for science.

THE RAGE TO MASTER: GIFTED CHILDREN HAVE IT, AND SO DO SUPERHEROES

Gifted children have a deep intrinsic motivation to master the domain in which they have high ability and are almost manic in their energy level.[24] Often, gifted children can't be torn away from activities in their area of giftedness, whether it involves an instrument, a computer, a sketch pad, or a math book. These children have a powerful interest in the domain in which they have high ability, and they can focus so intently on work in this domain that they lose sense of the outside world. They combine an obsessive interest with an ability to learn easily in a given domain. Unless social and emotional factors interfere, this combination leads to high achievement. This intrinsic drive is part and parcel of an exceptional, inborn giftedness.

This "rage to master" characterizes children we have traditionally labeled *gifted*: children with high IQs who excel in school. It also characterizes children we have traditionally classified as *talented*, children who excel in art, music, or athletics. This rage to master also characterizes superheroes. Young Bruce Wayne provides an apt example. After his parents' murders, he vowed to avenge their deaths by "warring on criminals" in his home city of Gotham City. He then proceeded to master the skills needed to make his vow a reality. He spent *hours* mastering the skills needed for the forensic analysis that is part of detecting, and additional *hours* mastering a variety of fighting techniques and martial arts, then *hours* maintaining and improving his physical fighting abilities, strength, and endurance. Not to mention the mental training necessary to become the Caped Crusader.

The intense drive characterizing gifted children should be recognized, celebrated, and cultivated, not destroyed. When children are not sufficiently challenged in school, as so often happens to gifted children, they sometimes lose their motivation and become underachievers. When parents and schools try to force single-minded, driven children to be well rounded by curtailing activity in the children's domain of giftedness and having the children spend time on more "normal" activities, they may end up stifling the children's drive. Imagine young Bruce Wayne forced by teachers or parents to spend less time on his detecting and athletic pursuits and more time on creative writing, on interacting with his peers (insisting, for example, that he play with other students on the playground instead of jogging the perimeter of the playground to build up his endurance). What would have become of him then? Or what if young Tony Stark's teachers had made him stop his inventing (or scribbling his ideas down) during class time—and forced him to study physics at the same pace as the rest of the students. Would he have still gone on to develop the Arc Reactor (as in the *Iron Man* film) or miniature transistors (as in the Iron Man comic, *Tales of Suspense* #37)? Might he have become an underachiever?

Which brings up the issue of the classroom. In addition to being bored and underchallenged in the classroom, it is well known that gifted children feel different from others and often try to hide their gifts and outwardly dumb themselves down for social acceptance. In contrast, some schools and school districts have special classrooms or programs for gifted children (the definition of "gifted" may vary somewhat from program to program, but usually it means an IQ score of at least 120). Admission to such programs is typically based on test scores as well as teacher recommendation.

In the X-Men world, students at Professor Xavier's School for Gifted Youngsters (later renamed the Xavier Academy) are in the mutant equivalent of a gifted program. Instead of taking a test to gain admission, though, Professor Charles Xavier (Professor X for short) uses his mutant abilities to locate children with mutant gifts and invites them to be students in his school. What he offers them is an opportunity to be with other gifted children, and a place where they need not hide their gifts.

Like gifted children in our world, every class at Professor X's school is composed of gifted children who each have a different profile of specific talents and abilities. Each gifted mutant, for instance, has different abilities; one might have phenomenal strength, another able to create fire, still another to turn water to ice, use telepathy, or any other myriad talents and combinations. In our world, the same is true of gifted children: Some gifted children are phenomenal at algebra, some are amazing writers, others have a deep understanding of chemistry that belies their years, or some combination of abilities. What the youngsters in Professor X's school and in gifted classrooms in our world have in common is an ability that is way beyond that of the typical student.

THE SOCIAL AND EMOTIONAL SIDE OF BEING AHEAD: GIFTED CHILDREN AND SUPERHEROES

The study of giftedness began in earnest in the early part of this century, when Lewis Terman initiated a large-scale longitudinal study of over 1,500 high-IQ children. The first volume of findings about this group appeared in 1925,[25] a 40-year follow-up appeared in 1968,[26] and a volume describing the survivors in their 80s appeared in 1995.[27] Terman's goal was to dispel the myth that gifted children are maladjusted and emotionally troubled. Terman tried to use his evidence to show that the participants in his study were, in his words, "superior to unselected children in physique, health and social adjustment; [and] marked by superior moral attitudes as measured by character tests of trait ratings."[28]

How did Terman select his "gifted" children? The first cut came from teacher nominations of the brightest children and also the youngest children in their classes. The youngest were chosen because of the possibility that children entering school early would be gifted. Nominated students who then scored in the top 1 percent of the school population on an intelligence test were admitted to the study. Students enrolled in the study also had their personality and social and emotional adjustment assessed; teachers rated students on a variety of scales. Terman reported that his students scored above average in social and emotional health, and thus he tried to dispel the myth of the gifted misfit. However, the teachers may well have been subject to a halo effect—perceiving the students they had nominated as gifted as being generally better on all dimensions. Thus many do not accept the conclusion that those with high IQ are socially and emotionally well adjusted. (In fact there is reason to believe that the higher the ability level, the less adjusted is the child, simply because this child does not fit in with most any social group.)

Leta Hollingworth, another early researcher of gifted children, was one who argued that children with gifts have social and emotional difficulties. She examined a subset of gifted children—those with profoundly high IQs (over 180)—and argued that such children had special social and emotional problems.[29] Hollingsworth's claim has since been substantiated: For instance, in a more recent report it was estimated that the rate of social and emotional difficulties experienced by profoundly academically gifted children is about twice the rate found among the nongifted, with almost a quarter of such children having such difficulties.[30] Extreme levels of giftedness lead to isolation. In the hopes of decreasing that isolation and becoming more popular, during middle childhood profoundly gifted children may try to hide their abilities—much as did many superheroes whose powers manifested during childhood. Young Charles Xavier and Clark Kent come to mind as examples. (Academically gifted girls are more apt to try to hide their gifts than are boys, and such girls report more depression, lower self-esteem, and more psychosomatic symptoms than do academically gifted boys.[31])

Social problems aren't limited to children whose gifts are in the academic realms. Teenagers with gifts in the visual arts, music, and athletics have as many difficulties with their peers as do those gifted in academic areas.[32] These teenagers have been shown to be atypical socially and emotionally in a number of respects: They are highly driven, nonconforming, and independent thinkers.

Not all gifted children want more social contact, though, and as noted earlier, only a minority of these children have social and emotional difficulties. As a rule, gifted children in all domains also tend to be introverted. They spend more time alone than do ordinary adolescents. They gain stimulation from themselves more than from others and report liking solitude far more than do most other people.[33] Although Tony Stark grew up to be a ladies man and was comfortable around people, as a child he spent significant amounts of time alone while experimenting and inventing. Bruce Wayne happily spent hours alone acquiring the knowledge and skills he'd need to become the Caped Crusader, and as an adult he seems more comfortable alone than with others. And Peter Parker definitely spent a lot of time alone as a child. Gifted children are solitary not only because of their rich inner lives, but also because solitude is requisite for the development of their talent. Whereas ordinary children come home after school to play, gifted children come home after school eager to paint, play music, work on math problems, read, or write—to engage in activities of their gifted domain.

The findings about solitude and socialization are somewhat paradoxical. One study showed that gifted adolescents like solitude more than do ordinary children, but also report a preference to be with others rather than be alone.[34] Thus, although they gain more from solitude than do others, they still yearn for peer contact. But it is difficult for these atypical children to find like-minded peers.

The desire for like-minded peers is one of the strongest arguments for placing gifted children in advanced classes. Imagine what it is like for a gifted mutant to be in a regular classroom, and have to hide his or her abilities, something that Professor X had to do with his ability to read minds (he could answer a teacher's question before it was asked).[35] Yet in a class with gifted peers, he wouldn't have to hide his ability, and could be with others who understood him.

In our world, advanced classes for gifted students—where they can be with similarly abled peers—are almost nonexistent at the elementary school level, infrequent at the middle school level, and common at the high school level. Such opportunities come in the form of honors classes, advanced placement classes, and college-level courses.

Advanced courses also exist in summer or weekend programs at many universities around the country.[36] Since 1979, over 100,000 students have participated in programs across the country now run by the Institute for the Academic Advancement of Youth at the Johns Hopkins University.[37] Students are selected on the basis of a high Scholastic Aptitude Test (SAT) or American College Testing (ACT) score earned as early as late elementary school. (Students also participate in various annual regional talent searches based on the same model. In some of these talent searches students all the way down to the second grade are tested using age-appropriate versions of the SAT and the ACT.) Students take courses in their area of high ability, and they find the experience to be very positive, particularly because meeting like-minded peers means they feel less isolated.[38] There are now about a dozen residential state-supported high schools for the gifted, as well as an equal number of residential early-entrance-to-college programs; these make it possible for highly gifted children to mix with equally gifted peers.[39] Professor X's vision of a school for gifted youngsters is becoming a reality.

GIFTED CHILDREN ARE NOT NECESSARILY CREATIVE. ARE SUPERHEROES?

Giftedness is not the same as creativity. We make a distinction between little-c creativity and big-C Creativity. Little-c creativity refers to doing something in a novel way, coming up with innovative approaches to problems, but not altering a domain of knowledge. Big-C Creativity refers to discoveries and innovations that fundamentally change a domain. Thus, Darwin's theory of evolution, Freud's invention of psychoanalysis, Picasso's and Braques's invention of cubism all qualify as instances of big-C creativity.

Most gifted children (including the *most* gifted, those we call child prodigies) do not go on to become big-C Creators. The children in Terman's study typically became experts—but not game-changers—in a well-established domain (e.g., medicine, law, business, academia). Although they may have been creative in the little-c sense, they did not become major creators. That is, they neither created a new domain nor revolutionized an old domain. And this is generally true of most superheroes as well: They have joined the ranks of superheroes, but they don't define or change what it means to be a superhero. Superman was the first superhero, and as such was a game-changer. He forged the path that others have followed.[40] One could argue that Tony Stark is a game-changer: He became more than just an expert in electrical and mechanical engineering; he invented revolutionary devices—the Arc Reactor in the films and miniature transistors in the comic books. Some people might make a similar argument about Bruce Wayne's various inventions for detecting and solving crimes. However, since he keeps his inventions—or the technology behind them—to himself, he doesn't revolutionize a field.

Expertise as an endpoint should not be lightly dismissed, though. Society needs experts, and we can neither expect nor hope that all prodigies will become creators. Many gifted children grow up to become happy and well-adjusted experts in their fields.

The path for the fraction of gifted children who eventually become revolutionary adult creators, like Tony Stark, can be painful, as they transition from a child prodigy (a child who learns rapidly and effortlessly in an established domain) to an adult creator (a person who disrupts and ultimately remakes a domain).[41]

It is not surprising that most gifted children, even most child prodigies, do not go on to become adult creators. All young children, whether typical or gifted, think divergently and engage in fantasy play. However, this kind of universal creative thinking is quite different from the kind of big-C Creativity that is involved in reshaping a domain. Individuals who are creative in this big-C sense have a personality structure different from that of the typical gifted (and nongifted) child: They are rebellious, they have a desire to alter the status quo, and they have often suffered childhoods of stress and trauma.[42] Their families are often a far cry from the complex families of engaged gifted adolescents.[43]

Although many superheroes had childhoods filled with stress and trauma, as a rule, they don't have the other characteristics of big-C Creators: they aren't typically rebellious (although they may be frustrated with the criminal justice system or police department) and they don't generally want to alter the status quo—other than decreasing crime and other nefarious deeds. Batman may want to shake up the criminals in Gotham City, but he doesn't want to shake up everything (at least not in most story lines). Even big-C Creator Tony Stark is only a Creator in the scientific realm, not in the superhero/justice realm. In fact, being a superhero is about maintaining the status quo—but one with fewer criminals. And although antiheroes may be rebellious, their rebellion is confined to taking justice into their own hands; they are rebelling against the criminal justice system as it is exercised in their home cities. Antiheroes aren't anarchists and don't want to shake up the entire city. They just want to prevent crimes and punish criminals—which doesn't always happen often enough for their tastes. Being a superhero really is about upholding the status quo—and so by definition, superheroes are not big-C Creators.

Our fascination with superheroes reflects our fascination with atypical children with astonishing gifts. Gifted children inspire envy and fear as well as admiration. We are threatened by seeing a child with abilities that outstrip our own. These children can make us feel slow. But we are also in awe of them because we cannot understand where their abilities came from. We seem to be less threatened by gifted adults (at least we are not being outdone by 6-year-olds!) and we simply classify them as in another world from our own. Gifted adults inspire more awe than envy—whether in sports, science, literature, or the arts. We can't compete with them and we know it (unless we're gifted too, and in the same domain!). Most of us accept that we are in a different class than gifted adults.

Perhaps we create and consume stories about superheroes both as an outlet for our admiration of the skills and achievements of gifted adults, and as a way to grapple with our envy of gifted children. Superheroes are so clearly not human—even the human ones—that we don't have to compare ourselves to them; they do not threaten us the way human gifted children do. We can instead admire them without any ambivalence.

NOTES

1. Feldman, D. H., & Goldsmith, L. T. (1991). *Nature's gambit: Child prodigies and the development of human potential.* New York: Teachers College Press.
   Radford, J. (1990). *Child prodigies and exceptional early experience.* London: Harvester. Winner, E. (1996). *Gifted children: Myths and realities.* New York: Basic Books.
2. Detterman, D., & Daniel, M. (1989). Correlations of mental tests with each other and with cognitive variables are highest for low IQ groups. *Intelligence, 15,* 349–359.
3. Wilkinson, S. C. (1993). WISC–R profiles of children with superior intellectual ability. *Gifted Child Quarterly, 37,* 84–91.
4. Achter, J., Lubinski, D., & Benbow, C. (1996). Multipotentiality among the intellectually gifted: "It was never there in the first place, and already it's vanishing." *Journal of Counseling Psychology, 43,* 65–76.
5. Benbow, C. P., & Minor, L. L. (1990). Cognitive profiles of verbally and mathematically precocious students: Implications for identification of the gifted. *Gifted Child Quarterly, 34,* 21–26.
6. Csikszentmihalyi, M., Rathunde, K., & Whalen, S. (1993). *Talented teenagers: The roots of success and failure.* New York: Cambridge University Press.
   Schellenberg, E. G. (2011). Examining the association between music lessons and intelligence. *British Journal of Psychology, 102,* 283–302.
7. Csikszentmihalyi, Rathunde, & Whalen (1993).
8. Ericsson, K. A., Krampe, R., & Tesch-Romer, C. (1993). The role of deliberate practice in the acquisition of expert performance. *Psychological Review, 100,* 363–406.
9. Csikszentmihalyi, M. (1996). *Creativity: Flow and the psychology of discovery and invention.* New York: HarperCollins.
   Gardner, H. (1993a). *Creating minds: An anatomy of creativity seen through the lives of Freud, Einstein, Picasso, Stravinsky, Eliot, Graham and Gandhi.* New York: Basic Books.

Gruber, H. (1981). *Darwin on man: A psychological study of scientific creativity* (2nd ed.). Chicago: University of Chicago Press.

10. Gruber, H. (1986). The self-construction of the extraordinary. In R. J. Sternberg & J. E. Davidson (Eds.), *Conceptions of giftedness* (pp. 247–263). Cambridge, UK: Cambridge University Press.
11. Roe, A. (1951). A psychological study of physical scientists. *Genetic Psychology Monograph, 43*(2), 121–235.
12. Bloom, B. (1985). *Developing talent in young people*. New York: Ballantine.
13. Ericsson, Krampe, & Tesch-Romer (1993).
14. Feldman & Goldsmith (1991); Winner (1996).
15. Bloom (1985); Roe (1951).
16. Diggle, A., & Jock. (2007). *Green Arrow: Year One*. New York: DC Comics.
17. VanTassel-Baska, J. L. (1989). Characteristics of the developmental path of eminent and gifted adults. In J. L. VanTassel-Baska & P. Olszewski-Kubilius (Eds.), *Patterns of influence on gifted learners: The home, the self, and the school* (pp. 146–162). New York: Teachers College Press.
18. Freeman, J. (1979). *Gifted children: Their identification and development in a social context*. Baltimore: University Park Press.
19. Csikszentmihalyi, Rathunde, & Whalen (1993).
20. Scarr, S., & McCartney, K. (1983). How people make their own environments: A theory of genotype–environment effects. *Child Development, 54,* 424–435.
21. Csikszentmihalyi, Rathunde, & Whalen (1993).
22. Goertzel, M. G., Goertzel, V., & Goertzel, T. G. (1978). *Three hundred eminent personalities*. San Francisco: Jossey-Bass.
23. Colangelo, N., & Dettman, D. G. (1983). A review of research on parents and families of gifted children. *Exceptional Children, 50,* 20–27. Terman, L. M., & Oden, M. H. (1947). *Genetic studies of genius: Vol. 4. The gifted child grows up*. Stanford, CA: Stanford University Press.
24. Winner (1996).

25. Terman, L. M. (1925). *Genetic studies of genius: Vol. 1. Mental and physical traits of a thousand gifted children*. Stanford, CA: Stanford University Press.
26. Oden, M. H. (1968). The fulfillment of promise: 40-year follow-up of the Terman gifted group. *Genetic Psychology Monographs, 77*(1), 3–93.
27. Holahan, C., & Sears, R. (1995). *The gifted group in later maturity*. Stanford, CA: Stanford University Press.
28. Subotnik, R., & Arnold, A. (Eds.). (1994). *Beyond Terman: Contemporary longitudinal studies of giftedness and talent*. Norwood, NJ: Ablex, pp. 17–18.
29. Hollingworth, L. (1942). *Children above 180 IQ, Stanford-Binet origin and development*. Yonkers, NY: World Book.
30. Janos, P., & Robinson, N. (1985). Psychosocial development in intellectually gifted children. In F. Horowitz & M. O'Brien (Eds.), *The gifted and talented: Developmental perspectives* (pp. 149–195). Washington, DC: American Psychological Association.
31. Gross, M. (1993). *Exceptionally gifted children*. London: Routledge.
32. Csikszentmihalyi, Rathunde, & Whalen (1993).
33. Csikszentmihalyi, Rathunde, & Whalen (1993).
34. Csikszentmihalyi, Rathunde, & Whalen (1993).
35. See Marvel's Uncanny X-Men #12.
36. Stanley, J. C. (1988). Some characteristics of SMPY's "700–800 on SAT-M before age 13 group": Youths who reason extremely well mathematically. *Gifted Child Quarterly, 32,* 205–209.
37. Johns Hopkins University. (1999). *Institute for the Academic Advancement of Youth: History, mission, and goals*. Baltimore: Author. Retrieved December 3, 1999, from http://www.jhu.edu.proxy.bc.edu/gifted/news/mission.html.
38. Benbow, C. P., & Lubinski, D. (1997). Intellectually talented children: How can we best meet their needs? In N. Colangelo & G. Davis (Eds.), *Handbook of gifted education* (2nd ed., pp. 155–169). Boston: Allyn & Bacon.
    Enersen, D. (1993). Summer residential programs: Academics and beyond. *Gifted Child Quarterly, 37,* 169–176.

39. Boothe, D., Sethna, B. W., Stanley, J. C., & Colgate, S. (1999). Special educational opportunities for able high school students: A description of residential early-college-entrance programs. *Journal of Secondary Gifted Education. Brain and Cognition, 10,* 195–202.
40. For a discussion of Superman as the first superhero, see Rosenberg R., & Coogan P. (2012). *What is a superhero?* Oxford, UK: Oxford University Press.
41. Gardner, H. (1993a).
    Gardner, H. (1993b). The relationship between early giftedness and later achievement. In G. R. Bock & K. Ackrill (Eds.), *The origins and development of high ability* (pp. 175–182). New York: Wiley.
    Simonton, D. K. (1994). *Greatness: Who makes history and why*. New York: Guilford Press.
42. Gardner, H. (1993a); Goertzel, Goertzel, & Goertzel (1978).
43. Csikszentmihalyi, Rathunde, & Whalen (1993).

EIGHT

The Very Real Work Lives of Superheroes

Illustrations of Work Psychology

Gary N. Burns and Megan B. Morris

Editor's Note

Most superheroes work double duty: They have the "job" of superhero as well as a civilian job. What is the nature of their relationship with both types of jobs? Gary Burns and Megan Morris bring their expertise in the psychology of job performance to address this question as they explore what motivates superheroes to do their jobs and the extent to which the stresses of their jobs are similar to jobs in our world. In other words, Burns and Morris explain superheroes' work lives and compare them with our work lives—and we can judge whether we'd really want their jobs.

—Robin S. Rosenberg

THE 9-TO-5 SIDE OF BEING A SUPERHERO

From their beginnings in the 1930s, the superheroes portrayed first in comics and later in feature films and television shows have fascinated our society. On the surface it is easy to guess at the appeal of these superheroes to modern readers and filmgoers. They are larger-than-life entities who stand time after time against the forces of injustice, chaos, and evil. However, if this was all they were, we would quickly tire of their exploits and move on to new characters and new stories. Aware of this, the authors of these stories embed their heroes with personalities and lives that are just as interesting as their adventures. One aspect of the modern superhero that both comic book readers and moviegoers can relate to is that of the superheroes' work life.

Despite superhero status, a surprising number of heroes have full-time employment outside of crime fighting and saving the world. One of the most famous examples is the mild-mannered reporter Clark Kent, who works diligently as a reporter for the *Daily Planet* when he isn't saving the world as Superman. Should we be surprised that Jerry Siegel and Joe Schuster, Superman's cocreators, would add such mundane details and give Clark Kent a day job? Clark Kent's job not only provided opportunity for character development, but it grounded Superman, an alien entity, with an aspect of life that most people could relate to.

While there are a number of superheroes, such as Captain America, who are actually employed as heroes, Superman isn't the only superhero with a day job. From billionaire industrialist Tony Stark to freelance photographer Peter Parker, a whole host of superheroes and supervillains incorporate regular human jobs into their daily identities. Their everyday experiences, as envisioned by their creators, have been captured on the comic book page beside the heroic feats. With Superman, this tactic might have been to ground an alien in American culture, but it was a technique that many writers realized they could use. Not only was work something that readers could relate to, it was a way of providing character development outside of dramatic action. But how realistic are the views of the workplace and the problems that the superhero employee faces in these stories? In this chapter, we will examine the images of superhero work life and compare it to research on the workplace and work behavior to determine whether these aspects of our superheroes are just fiction—or if they reflect the same dynamics and dilemmas that we ourselves face.

THE STUDY OF WORK

Our jobs are such an important part of our lives that entire professions are dedicated to studying and learning about behavior at work. Fields such as *industrial and organizational psychology* focus on examining a wide range of different aspects of the workforce, both from the perspective of the employer and from the view of the employee. This field focuses on the application of management and psychological principles in organizational and work settings and assumes a data driven approach to answering the questions that trouble employers. For companies, this is valuable because of the scientific techniques applied to understanding the nature of work and identifying the root causes of problems, not just the symptoms. Common practices that these psychologists engage in include examining the nature of jobs, testing the accuracy and fairness of hiring programs, evaluating training programs, improving the accuracy of performance appraisals, and managing employee turnover.

At its heart, the field of industrial and organizational psychology is the science of people at work. One aspect of this is the investigation of what motivates and challenges people to excel in the workplace. For example, such factors as job satisfaction and autonomy at work, among others, motivate and challenge people. Researchers also seek to understand the impact of the negative aspects of the work environment. Examples range from understanding the root causes of violence in the workplace to the impact of abusive supervision on employee health and morale. In this way, industrial and organizational psychology focuses on improving both the organization's bottom line and the work environment of the employee. The field has been growing almost constantly over the last century in the United States and across the industrialized world. Despite the relatively minor number of psychologists in this field, only about 4 percent of all psychologists, it has grown to be one of the major applied sciences in psychology and business worldwide.

Using principals of industrial and organizational psychology, we hope to answer two questions. First, why do superheroes work? What are the forces that drive superheroes either to take a job wearing spandex or to seek out a secondary 9-to-5 job? Second, is the stress that superheroes experience in the workplace realistic or is it just fiction? Specifically, what is the cost of work on our lives (and superhero lives) and how are the symptoms of work stress viewed in superhero stories? The overall purpose of this chapter is to bring attention to the scientific study of work by examining how these principles are reflected in the stories we surround ourselves with.

WHY DO SUPERHEROES WORK?

To answer the question of why superheroes work, we first want to explore the types of jobs that superheroes have and distinguish different types of working superheroes. Then, we can review the relevant theories of work motivation that will inform our discussion of why superheroes work, with examples from comics and movies.

When picturing the working life of superheroes, the stories that most often come to mind are those of Superman and Spider-Man. Both are hugely popular superheroes with commercially successful movies and thousands of printed pages devoted to their stories. Both also have 9-to-5 jobs that are separate from their heroic exploits. Superman, as Clark Kent, spends a good part of his day behind a desk trying to land interviews while facing menacing story deadlines. When not slinging webs, Peter Parker is a freelance photographer trying to make enough money to support himself and care for his elderly aunt. Other examples of superheroes with day jobs include the lawyers Matt Murdock (Daredevil) and Jennifer Walters (She-Hulk) and the scientists Ted Kord (Blue Beetle), Barry Allen (The Flash), and Ray Palmer (The Atom). A superhero's motive for holding down a second job ranges from a need for money to a need to maintain a nonhero connection with society.

However, not all superheroes want or need the second job. Many are able to make their incomes through their roles in society as professional superheroes. Heroes in this category include such notables as Marvel's Luke Cage (Power Man) and DC's Booster Gold,[1] as well as many more. Perhaps the most famous example of such a character is Captain America, who was originally a soldier in the employment of the United States during World War II. Often, these heroes are part of a larger team sponsored by private corporations or by governments. For example, since their creation in the 1960s, the Avengers have been a professional superhero group fighting together to defeat enemies and threats that were beyond any single superhero. As developed by writer Roy Thomas, the Avengers were funded by founding member Iron Man, through his identity of Tony Stark and the Maria Stark Foundation. The Avengers are an interesting example because although they are financially backed by a private corporation, they have won approval from the National Security Council of the United States and the General Assembly of the United Nations. In contrast, other superhero teams such as the Watchmen are considered outlaws and vigilantes, lacking approval from the authorities. Other popular examples of professional teams include the Justice Society of America, Stormwatch,[2] the Fantastic Four, and Hellboy's investigation team at the Bureau for Paranormal Research and Defense. Teamwork is an important aspect of crime-fighting groups, but it's also an important aspect in everyday work. Whether it's being a part of a think tank or just working with coworkers to meet a project deadline, teamwork is a central component to the workplace.

What motivates these superheroes to take on the role of a "worker," either in secondary jobs or as professional superheroes?

While a full analysis of the work identity of superheroes is beyond the scope of this essay, it is possible to apply some key motivational theories to these superheroes and their work. Within psychology, motivation is typically discussed as the internal force that initiates, guides, and maintains human behavior. Motivation plays a major role in the study of work behavior, and researchers have developed a number of theories to explain why people engage in different tasks. For our purposes, we break down these theories into two different types: needs theories and cognitive theories.

One of the most iconic and well known theories of motivation is Maslow's hierarchy of needs.[3] Maslow described a pyramid of needs, with each stage achievable only after the previous level's needs had been satisfied. At the bottom are physiological needs, such as food, water, and sleep. Next are safety and love needs. Beyond these are growth needs, such as esteem—the need for feeling confident and gaining the respect of others. At the tip of Maslow's pyramid is self-actualization, which, according to his theory, many people will never realize.

Borrowing from this legacy, many motivational theories use the hierarchy of needs as a starting point. Maslow's theory is considered a needs theory because it holds that humans have certain basic needs and when these needs are not met, people are driven to fulfill them. Maslow's theory is different from other needs theories because he included both physical needs, such as for food and shelter, as well as social and psychological needs, such as a need for belonging and the need for self-respect. Maslow argued that these basic physiological and safety needs must be met before people are motivated by higher level needs.

While the strict hierarchy that Maslow described isn't supported by research, it represents a starting structure to understand the complex needs that motivate superheroes to engage in work. In the fictional framework of these superhero stories, being able to present different human needs provides character development and complexity. Is it any wonder that the most well known of these stories reflect aspects that we can relate to, even if only abstractly? Spider-Man is a great example of a superhero forced to seek out an additional job. As presented in Sam Raimi's 2002 movie *Spider-Man*, Peter Parker fights crime in disguise to make up for his failure to save his uncle Ben. But being a do-gooder doesn't pay the bills—and because of Peter's elderly Aunt May's health care, the Parker family has several bills to pay. Instead of turning his powers to villainy to gain ill-gotten riches, he picks up a freelance position with the *Daily Bugle* as a photographer and becomes especially well known for his shots of Spider-Man. Why did Parker choose the path he did? Imagine, if you will, police cars chasing a get-away car carrying bank robbers between city high-rises while our hero follows above, swinging from web to web. The robbers come to their destination point, but are soon surprised by the web-slinger. When the police find the robbers they are tied together with web and all the money is missing. In this case Spider-Man is making a living through theft, a shameful and disrespectful act. This would be especially shameful to Peter, since the man who murdered his uncle Ben was a common thief.

While we might be interested in hearing a story about a morally ambiguous superhero, that isn't the story of Spider-Man. These actions would change the character, and thus the story. Given that these actions are representations of the character, Maslow's hierarchy provides a model for representing the character's needs. While it would have been easy for Spider-Man to illegally or immorally gather the funds he needs, Peter chooses a different path. As we will explore here, Maslow's hierarchy provides a model for understanding Peter's sense of responsibility as he works hard to provide for his sick aunt while attempting to balance his life as a superhero.

This perspective on Spider-Man illustrates the different levels of Maslow's hierarchy and yet also illustrates the critiques researchers have lobbed at the theory. On the one hand, Spider-Man works as a freelance photographer to fulfill both physiological and safety needs. That is, he is paying the bills to provide himself with food and shelter. More than simply surviving, though, Spider-Man is also providing for his Aunt May, which maintains his needs for love, affection, and esteem. But of course, while Maslow's theory helps us understand human needs, as we see here and can easily imagine in ourselves, needs do not ascend up a rigid hierarchy. It's more complicated than that. In fact, humans often have needs that run counter to one another. Consider someone dieting for the sole purpose of becoming thinner. Under such a strict hierarchy as Maslow's, it would be impossible to balance basic dietary needs and the need to fit some societal standard.

Maslow's hierarchy aside, one general problem with needs theories of motivation is that they attempt to explain why humans must act. Peter Parker *must* work to take care of his family's basic needs. Matt Murdock *must* be both a lawyer and Daredevil because of his need to provide justice. Superman *must* have a secret identity because of his need for normal social interaction. While needs theories explain why activities are initiated, they don't explain why people engage in specific behaviors in specific situations to obtain specific outcomes. If Superman has a need for love and belonging, why does he choose to take a job as a reporter? He could have just as easily satisfied those needs as a customer service representative. To answer these types of questions we must consider cognitive theories of motivation.

Cognitive theories of motivation focus on why individuals choose to engage in specific behaviors under specific situations. Research examining cognitive theories often focus on goal-setting theory, need for achievement, and the need for meaningfulness in work. Of these theories, goal-setting theory has received the most research and is currently recognized as one of the most widely used and practically important theories in use today.[4]

Research on goal-setting theory has found that individuals with goals typically perform at higher levels than individuals without goals.[5] There are two broad reasons why goal setting is so powerful. First, an individual's goals provide specific information about what he or she is trying to achieve, allowing the individual to identify specific behaviors that will bring the goal closer. Second, knowing a goal is reachable provides immediate feedback about progress toward meeting the goal. Individuals can easily assess whether they have met their goal, or if they need to strive harder or try something different. Research in industrial and organizational psychology has found that self-set goals are the most powerful, but even goals set by supervisors can improve organizational performance. Furthermore, for goals to be most effective, they should be specific, measurable, attainable, realistic, and time sensitive. To the extent that goals conform to these guidelines, they will better specify what behavior will be most effective and provide feedback to help people attain their goals.

Most goal-directed behavior among superheroes is not directed toward the jobs themselves, but toward the plot of the story being told. However, the authors of these stories have incorporated other elements of goal-directed behaviors that serve to motivate superheroes at work. Most superheroes have a strong need for achievement, which in this context refers to an individual's desire to make a significant accomplishment, to master skills, and to have high standards of accomplishment. In stories, superheroes are often shown with a need for achievement as well as a desire to seek meaningfulness in work, both of which combine needs theories and cognitive theories of motivation.

A great example of the motivating potential of these traits can be seen with Superman who, despite his alien background, was raised in the Midwestern United States. As such, his view of work is typical of the general American culture's view of work. In American society work is often an important aspect of *the American dream*, the opportunity for prosperity and success regardless of social class or circumstances of birth. For many, it's also important to have a job in order to gain a respectful status among your peers. No one can deny that Clark Kent is one hell of a reporter, but to fully understand why Superman spends a good part of his working life behind a desk or trying to pin down an interview, we need to take a closer look at his job as a reporter at *The Daily Planet*, one of Metropolis's premier papers. There are many differences across the Superman mythos, but each version assumes that the outwardly shy and awkward Kent is hired as an investigative reporter at this prestigious paper. Mark Waid's retelling of the Superman story in *Superman Birthright* presents many images of how Superman views his work as a reporter. Consider the dialogue below as Superman's adoptive parents question him about his career choice:

JONATHAN KENT: "That said, are you sure surrounding yourself with reporters is the smartest career move?"

CLARK KENT: "I'm a journalist, Pa. And I'm **good** at it. Besides, working in a newsroom means I'm first to hear when I'm...you know... needed."[6]

Later in Waid's saga, Superman's choice of a career is questioned again—by Editor-in-chief Perry White during his initial interview. Referencing Clark Kent's mild manners, Perry asks why he isn't a bank teller instead of a reporter. Superman tells the truth: "Because, Mr. White, you have the fastest, most reliable news service in the world. Whenever a story happens, the *Planet* gets it first and has it webbed and in print while the *New York Times* is still fishing for sources. Your staff is that good. And I'm that good."[7]

It makes sense that Superman would want to be in a position of achievement—not only at the most prestigious newspaper, but at an organization that truly excels in what it does. Twice he expresses that not only is he a journalist, but a *good* one too. This illustrates that Superman has a relatively high need for achievement, striving for meaningfulness in both his work as a superhero and as a reporter. As a journalist Superman can continue to fight for the innocent by spreading truth, as a result creating meaningfulness in his work. This quest for meaningfulness in work is one that we can identify with and is shared by millions of workers across the world. Fitting these images of our superheroes almost perfectly, the theory of interpersonal sensemaking by Amy Wrzesniewski, Jane Dutton, and Gelaye Debebe[8] presents a model explaining how our perceptions of our work, our coworkers, and ourselves impact meaningfulness and how meaningfulness is related to a number of positive feelings about both ourselves and our work.

The research on interpersonal sensemaking illustrates that while the nature of our work impacts its meaningfulness, individuals often shape their own jobs to enhance the meaningfulness they experience.[9] For instance, an individual might ask his or her supervisor for additional tasks to complete independently of other coworkers. As a result, the individual's work becomes more autonomous and valuable to that employee, enhancing the meaningfulness of that job. These implications are actually quite profound, indicating that perceptions of our work environment are really more important than the objective reality in determining meaningfulness, with each of us being capable of recognizing the important and interesting aspects of our work lives. One reason why this is so important is that a lack of meaningfulness in the workplace has been associated with increased feelings of stress,[10] a topic that we turn to next.

WOES OF THE WORKING HERO

Another aspect of a superhero's work life that most people can identify with is the stress involved. While they might not have to worry about defending humanity against oppressive forces of evil, nearly 75 percent of workers in the United States find their work stressful,[11] and 42 percent report that their work interferes with their personal lives.[12] Within the workplace, there are many sources of stress that employees must deal with ranging from daily, trivial hassles to hostile work environments. Although research has found that there are huge differences in what people find stressful, the resulting strains, or undesirable personal outcomes, are very similar.

The strains caused by stress typically manifest in three different forms. One of the most publicized and troubling forms is that of physical symptoms and illness, most notably cardiovascular problems. In a review of the published literature, researchers in Finland estimated that individuals working in a stressful environment had a 50-percent greater risk of coronary heart disease than workers who did not find their jobs stressful.[13] While it is uncommon to see superheroes suffering from such a serious medical strain, our heroes often can be seen experiencing what we refer to as either psychological or behavioral strains. Psychological strains—such as depression, anger, and anxiety—are insidious, as their onset is often gradual and the first signs of these strains are not obvious to the casual observer. Another psychological strain that is commonly associated with stress in the workplace is burnout, which will be discussed in more detail below. As if psychological strains weren't enough, these psychological problems are often linked back to physical illness as well, adding to the effects of stress in the workplace. Behavioral strains, which stem from psychological strains, typically manifest themselves as increased drinking, smoking, or violent behavior. Perhaps the best example of this type of strain can be seen in the Jon Favreau's 2010 *Iron Man 2* film, where the stress facing Tony Stark drives him deeper and deeper into the bottle. In this drunken state he even pilots the Iron Man suit, putting himself and numerous others at risk. An example of behavioral strain that manifests as violence is seen in Christopher Nolan's 2008 *The Dark Knight* during an interrogation in the police station between Batman and the Joker. While Batman is trying to find the whereabouts of Harvey Dent, the Joker tries to manipulate Batman by telling the Caped Crusader that he is a freak just like the Joker, and that soon Gotham City will no longer need Batman. This enrages Batman, and Batman, uncharacteristically, viciously beats the Joker. On both the screen and page, there are multitudes of heroes who experience and mirror these types of strains.

Given that a large portion of the working population experiences these stressors and strains, it shouldn't be surprising that we can identify with the problems facing superheroes in their own work lives. Here, let's examine three common types of stressors seen in superhero stories and some of the strains that are associated with them. These strains and the burnout that is often portrayed have caused almost as many woes and downfalls in heroes' lives as have the villains they face.

The first stressor that is commonly portrayed among our superheroes is social or self-directed pressure to perform. The pressure to perform is quite high on all superheroes, but it is different for those who also have professional careers. Not only do they have to consider the lives lost when they fail to meet expectations, but in some cases their jobs and futures as well. As presented in Mark Miller's *The Ultimates*, a gritty reimagining of the Avengers story, pressure to perform can be seen as the downfall for at least two of the team members: both Bruce Banner and Henry "Hank" Pym crumble under the pressures of the job. Here's what happens. After watching batch after batch of supersoldier serum fail to meet specifications, Banner finally injects himself to test its efficiency, thus creating the character of the Hulk, whose rampage kills hundreds of innocent bystanders. Pym, as the remaining scientist superhero, must continually strive to make both technological and heroic advances for the team, thus fulfilling his role and making up for Banner's absence. Unfortunately, while he continues to reinvent himself from Giant-Man to Ant-Man, the stress causes him to lose both his wife and his job.

Another common stressor that we can often relate to in our superhero stories is that of abusive supervision (think abusive bosses). Much of the research on leadership in the behavioral sciences has focused on ways that leaders motivate and inspire their employees. However, this research has also revealed a dark side of leadership that many of us already knew as fact—that abusive supervision is a prevalent problem. It is estimated that nearly 14 percent of workers are affected by abusive supervision, which costs US organizations a combined $23.8 billion annually in absenteeism, health care costs, and lost productivity.[14] These statistics indicate that not only is this a problem for the employees being harassed, but that the abusive nature of some supervisor relationships is extremely costly to the corporate world.

Among superheroes, the most visible examples of abusive supervision can be seen in the Spider-Man and Superman stories. In both superheroes' stories, our protagonists have to contend with overly hostile editors who rain down verbal abuse regarding deadlines. Less well known but equally revealing is the abusive supervision seen in the 1960s T.H.U.N.D.E.R. Agents (Tower Comics). Hired by the United Nations, these agents punch the clock, file reports, and deal with demanding managers more concerned about their superhero gadgets and deadlines than the heroes' health and safety. Taking it to an even further extreme, writer/creator Robert Kirkman shows the teenage superhero Invincible (Image Comics) being physically abused by his government boss—a situation that he would never have been able to escape without his superpowers. Even these powerful, heroic superheroes experience the too familiar feelings of worthlessness and weakness. Perhaps the authors included these aspects to show that these superheroes are not completely invulnerable, but much like the average person, experience the pains and restrictions of authority.

A final group of stressors seen in superhero stories can be examined in terms of role theory. Role theory is a social psychology theory that holds that each of us acts out a socially and personally defined set of roles. Examples of such roles include mother, manager, teacher, or even hero. To make things even more complex, we each have multiple roles that we seek to fulfill. For example, most workers in the industrialized world have to balance their roles as workers with their roles as spouses or students—and likely many more. Industrial and organizational psychology is interested in role theory for a variety of reasons, but one is the impact of *role conflict*, which occurs when there is disagreement between the goals of two or more of our roles. Consider the employee who has to work the afternoon shift to meet her responsibilities as a worker and family supporter; however, her role within her family is to spend this time at home with her family. This employee would now be facing role conflict. Superman sometimes experiences role conflict when the demands of his job as a superhero ("save that child about to be hit by the out-of-control car *now*") conflict with his role as Clark Kent, reporter ("I'm in the middle of this interview—how can I get away to save that child?").

Role conflict predicts many of the physical, psychological, and behavioral strains mentioned above, but has also been linked to withdrawal behavior, which can range from increased absenteeism, intentions to quit, and actual turnover. Peter Parker, for example, struggles constantly with role conflict that leads to withdrawal behavior. Known commonly as Spider-Man, Peter must also balance his role of superhero with that of worker/family supporter, boyfriend, and student. In the 2004 movie, *Spider-Man 2*, Peter is told by a doctor that the physical problems he has been having are due to mental stress. True to this analysis, we see Peter lose his superpowers; frustrated, he quits the superhero business. Within the Spider-Man comics, it is even more common for Spider-Man to withdraw, with this pattern also becoming a common theme over decades. We can find another example of role conflict in Christopher Nolan's 2005 film *Batman Begins*. Near the end of the film Rachel, Batman's love interest, explains that Bruce's current true self is Batman and that maybe one day she'll see the real Bruce again when "Gotham no longer needs Batman."

Other role stressors that afflict both ourselves and superheroes are *role ambiguity*, or a lack of clear expectations, and *role overload*, or an imbalance in work expectations (see pressure to perform above). We can find examples of both of these instances in Martin Campbell's 2011 film, *Green Lantern*. Hal Jordan, the Green Lantern, at first suffers from role ambiguity; he is not sure why the ring chooses him. The ring was supposed to choose an individual who is fearless. Hal has fears and doesn't believe he deserves the ring, leading to his problems early in the film.

In addition, Hal suffers from role overload; he doesn't believe he can live up to the expectations of the Green Lantern Intergalactic Corps. As a result, he quits training as a Green Lantern and heads back to Earth.

Instances of withdrawal, found in examples with Spider-Man and the Green Lantern, could also be characteristic of burnout, which has been shown to be related to role conflict, ambiguity, and overload. "Burnout" is the psychological term for the experience of work-related long-term exhaustion, diminished interest in a topic, and withdrawal. The symptoms of burnout are common throughout the world and are estimated to affect thousands, if not millions, of workers. Although burnout is often discussed as a single phenomenon, it actually consists of at least three components, any of which might be stronger than the others.[15] The component that receives the most research attention is that of exhaustion, both mental and physical. Individuals experiencing burnout are often in a constant state of exhaustion when it comes to their work lives, with even the thought of their work duties tiring them unreasonably. Another component of burnout that is often seen in our superhero stories is that of *depersonalization*, in which workers become very cynical about their work, with their perceptions of the workplace becoming very mechanical. For instance, superheroes experiencing this aspect of burnout are likely to lose sight of why they became heroes, viewing the people they save as just numbers and objects.

The final component of burnout is that of reduced personal accomplishment, or *inefficacy*, in which the suffering individual loses confidence in his or her own abilities to be successful. With this flagging confidence, the motivation to work—that we discussed earlier—crumbles, creating a downward spiral. In the stories of Spider-Man, it is most likely this component of burnout that Parker is experiencing most strongly. Moreover, as shown in the film *Spider-Man 2*, this downward spiral can increase rapidly with small initial failures further compounding the effects of burnout. It is not until Parker realizes that he is the only one capable of stopping Dr. Octopus that he overcomes this strain of failures and takes up his superhero mantle again. However, for those who think they can simply shake the effects of burnout like Spider-Man, consider the numerous other lesser known heroes who have failed to overcome this stress and abandoned the superhero aspects of their identity, such as Marvel's Wonder Man and Shang-Chi.[16]

CONCLUSION

It is not uncommon for superhero stories to contain elements of the heroes' work lives, both as superheroes and as traditional "9-to-5" employees. These recognizable elements make the superheroes relatable. Furthermore, as we've reviewed here, the authors of these stories have stayed remarkably true to the scientific research on motivation and stress in the workplace. At first glance, this might be surprising. After all, these characters are the essence of fiction, representing powers and situations that we can only dream of. Yet superhero writers have been able to instill in these characters the same daily trials in their work lives that we face and that scores of scientists are trying to better understand. An important lesson can be learned from many of these heroes' work lives and is especially illustrated by Superman: The quest for meaningfulness in our work lives can never be a failure if we sincerely begin that quest. Although our primary motivation to work might be to provide for basic human needs, the quest for meaningfulness can provide additional motivation and fulfillment in our work commitments and help protect us from the effects of stress in the workplace.

NOTES

1. *Editor's Note:* Luke Cage earns money as a "hero for hire," and Booster Gold earns money from corporate sponsors.
2. *Editor's Note:* Stormwatch is a superhero team sponsored by the United Nations and featured in Wildstorm comics.

3. Maslow, A. H. (1943). A theory of human motivation. *Psychological Review, 50,* 370–396.
4. Latham, G. P., & Pinder, C. C. (2005). Work motivation theory and research at the dawn of the twenty-first century. *Annual Review of Psychology, 56,* 485–516.
5. For a review of this work see Latham, G. P. (2007). *Work motivation: History, theory, research, and practice*. Thousand Oaks, CA: Sage.
6. Waid, M. (2005). *Superman birthright*. London: Titan, p. 85, emphasis added.
7. Waid (2005), p. 95.
8. Wrzesniewski, A., Dutton, J. E., & Debebe, G. (2003). Interpersonal sensemaking and the meaning of work. In R. M. Kramer & B. M. Staw (Eds.), *Research in organizational behavior: An annual series of analytical essays and critical reviews* (pp. 93–135). Oxford, UK: Elsevier.
9. Wrzesniewski, A., & Dutton, J. E. (2001). Crafting a job: Revisioning employees as active crafters of their work. *Academy of Management Review, 26,* 179–201.
10. Ahghar, G. (2008). The role of school organizational climate in occupational stress among secondary school teachers in Tehran. *International Journal of Occupational Medicine and Environmental Health, 21,* 319–329.
11. Smith, M. (2003, January). Employee health affects more than the bottom line. *IPMA News,* 8–10.
12. Gregg, L. (1998, September). Humanity in the workplace: When work/family becomes an HR issue. *Credit Union Executive*. Available online at http://www.highbeam.com/doc/1G1-54102403.html [January 5, 2011].
13. Kivimäki, M., Virtanen, M., Elovainio, M., Kouvonen, A., Väänänen, A., & Vahtera, J. (2006). Work stress in the etiology of

coronary heart disease—A meta-analysis. *Scandinavian Journal of Work, Environment and Health, 32,* 431–442.

14. Tepper, B. J., Duffy, M. K., Henle, C. A., Lambert, L. S. (2006). Procedural injustice, victim precipitation, and abusive supervision. *Personnel Psychology, 59,* 101–123.
15. Maslach, C. (1982). *Burnout: The cost of caring*. New York: Prentice-Hall.
16. *Editor's Note:* Wonder Man originally worked with the Avengers but did have his own comic from 1991–1994. Throughout Marvel's history he has actually quit several groups, making his history a tangle. Shang-Chi is presented in the Master of Kung Fu titles and numerous crossovers. He quit and retired as a fisherman, although he too was recycled years later and made additional guest appearances.

NINE

How Super Are Superheroes?

Robert J. Sternberg

EDITOR'S NOTE

Superheroes are not invulnerable. Not even Superman. And even smart superheroes can do stupid things (just like humans!). Using his expertise about intelligence, Robert Sternberg distills the wisdom and ethics that superheroes possess, the common psychological failings of supervillains, and how these characteristics exist not only in superheroes' worlds, but in our world too.

—Robin S. Rosenberg

I learned how to read from comic books about superheroes. I especially liked the Justice League of America, composed of Superman, Batman, Wonder Woman, Flash, Green Lantern, Aquaman, and J'onn J'onzz, Manhunter from Mars. I am eternally grateful to the comic-book industry, in general, and to the Justice League of America, in particular, for teaching me how to read. My greatest gratitude is to American Comics Group's *Forbidden Worlds*, my favorite of all. In the 1950s, the basal readers were about Dick, Jane, and Sally, and it would have been hard for their authors to craft more boring stories if they tried. But, in retrospect, I realize I learned far more than how to read from superhero comics—I just didn't learn what I learned until recently. I learned that the essence of superheroes was not in their physical powers but in their wisdom and ethical stance.

If one wants truly to understand superheroes, one needs to see the movie *Hancock*. The movie is about a man with superpowers who is anything but heroic and is notably lacking in wisdom and ethics. The protagonist of the movie has superpowers but he is a klutz and a jerk. He is, if anything, an antihero. Hancock has nothing to teach anyone, except for the vacuity of a superpowered individual who falls short of the ethical and behavioral standards expected even for the common man.

Hancock is important because he shows that superpowers in the absence of heroic dimensions of character fall flat. They fail to impress—at least, movie audiences. The lesson is that one needs more than superpowers to become a role model from whom young people can learn lessons. So what are the lessons one can learn from the true superheroes?

The essence of a superhero is in his or her wisdom and ethics, not in the superpowers. Superman, Batman, and all the members of the Justice League of America use their superpowers for good. Their antagonists are not amoral dingbats such as Hancock, but rather supervillains such as Lex Luthor, the Joker, the Mad Hatter, and Dr. Doom. These villains may or may not have super physical powers, but their combination of diabolical ingenuity and will to perpetrate evil renders them worthy foes of the superheroes. Not all superheroes really have super physical powers either. The Shadow, in reality Lamont Cranston, learned in the Far East how to use hypnotism to render himself invisible to those around him. But his powers are not deemed in the stories as super, but rather as available to anyone who happens to have the good fortune to run into a Far Eastern mentor with knowledge regarding hypnotism in the service of invisibility. What distinguishes the Shadow is his powerful motivation to use his newfound abilities to prove to all that "crime does not pay. The Shadow knows!"

The importance of wisdom and striving for good might be less important were it not for the fact that American schools today have essentially dispensed with the development of wisdom and ethics as part of the formal curriculum. The McGuffey readers of yore were designed to teach powerful lessons about ethics and about behavior that is good and right. But the advent of postmodernism—often construed to mean that any interpretation of anything can be justified—combined with the societal pressure of the No Child Left Behind Act—have left positive character development in the dust. One might like to believe that children would develop such characteristics on their own. But the evidence from our society is not promising: The economic fiasco of 2008, in which Wall Street bankers and their cronies almost brought down the entire US economy—does not speak well for the positive influence of the elite educations that the bankers and many of the politicians who supported them received. Lehman Brothers and all the failed banks of 2008–2010—the list is enormous (http://www.fdic.gov/bank/individual/failed/banklist.html)—were run by people who were well educated in a conventional sense. But clearly something was grossly missing from their educations—the development of wisdom.

Wisdom can be viewed as the use of one's skills and knowledge for a common good, over the long as well as the short term, through the infusion of positive ethical values. To address the major problems of the world, in general, and the United States, in particular, requires wisdom, not merely narrow intelligence and the knowledge that results from an elite education. It is depressing to know that, in the 20th century, IQs rose an average of 3 points every 10 years, and yet people are as susceptible to irrationality as ever. Whatever IQ represents, it is not intelligence or wisdom in any broad sense.

The US elections of 2010 were depressing in the appeals of politicians to emotion at the expense of reason. Some of the more extreme candidates who seemed rationality-challenged—Sharron Angle and Christine McDonnell—lost, but others who were almost as extreme won. Perhaps schools need to emphasize the wise thinking exemplified by superheroes rather than the vapid memory feats of quiz-show contestants who contribute through their knowledge to entertainment but not to the betterment of the world.

Although ordinary people cannot hope to be superheroes, they can come close. For me, personally, the most interesting of the superheroes is The Shadow, precisely because he accomplishes the ideal: to accomplish the maximum amount of good with the minimum amount of superpower. He is basically an ordinary person with useful training. Unlike many of the other superheroes, he is not from some other planet, never was bitten by a radioactive spider or by anything else, and has no real superpowers. Rather, as noted earlier, he simply has learned to hypnotize others so as to render himself invisible. He has no weakness such as kryptonite or flame, but anyone who can avoid seeing him can avoid his hypnotism. So he needs to take great care because his power is so limited.

What makes him so appealing is that in addition to being a "man about town," in which he is similar to Bruce Wayne (the alter ego of Batman), he is a psychologist and understands how people's guilty consciences can be made to work against them. He battles not supervillains but rather ordinary people with typical human frailties. He often will convince people to confess to their crimes because they cannot withstand the psychological pressure his role as The Shadow puts on them. In ordinary life, Lamont Cranston as The Shadow is nothing more than an ordinary citizen who understands what "evil lurks in the hearts of man" and believes that "Crime does not pay—The Shadow knows."

In a sense, Superman is perhaps the most challenging superhero because he is almost the opposite of The Shadow: His powers are close to unlimited. This must have made him a challenge to write about because there is so little he cannot do. When someone has so much power, it is hard to write an exciting story. But Superman raises an interesting and somewhat perplexing question: If he could do so much, why, in the grand scheme of things, did he do so little?

Superman, of course, battled ordinary villains and supervillains alike. In the early (1950s) television shows with George Reeves, Superman was depicted fighting quite ordinary villains. In the Superman movies (late 1970s and early 1980s) with Christopher Reeve, Superman battled villains who, in some cases, had powers comparable to his. But he was still basically a crime fighter, although on a larger scale. At various times in the history of Superman comics, Superman's powers varied, but he always had mental powers that far exceeded the ordinary, and at the best of times he had super mental powers. So one wonders why he was spending most of his time battling ordinary villains rather than using his super mental powers to find a cure for cancer, help achieve world peace, or bring down a few dictators who have caused immense suffering to the people beholden to them.

In short, Superman had a rather local focus, first as a boy in Smallville and then as a man in Metropolis. He mostly combated local crime, except perhaps in his key role in the Justice League of America, where nevertheless he was still a crime fighter. Was the vision of his creators too limited, or do the kinds of powers Superman had, including his mental ones, leave one with a curious narrowness of scope? Perhaps what was lacking in the education of Superman and most of the other superheroes was the kind of global focus that could have led them more to concentrate on problems of international scope that arguably needed their attention more than many of the local problems to which they attended.

The superheroes had other limitations, of course, that had nothing to do with Kryptonite or flame and the like. Superman illustrated these problems in his youthful attraction to Lana Lang and his later attractions to Lois Lane and Lori Lemaris (the mermaid). These attractions showed that, at least when it came to romance, he had all the problems everyone else has. Indeed, he had even greater problems, because he seemed so tied to the initials L. L. Spider-Man had romantic problems as well with Mary Jane. Bruce Wayne, aka Batman, lost Julie Madison to European royalty, who doubtless were less interesting than he was. Apparently having superpowers is no cure-all for problems of romance. Indeed, Clark Kent was plagued by his own alter ego: Lois Lane was interested in him as Superman but not as Clark. As Clark, he was personally vulnerable, but as Superman, he had other physical vulnerabilities.

Many of the superheroes are revealed to have a vulnerability. Superman has a vulnerability to kryptonite. Because of his great powers, he needs multiple vulnerabilities. Green kryptonite causes Superman to weaken and possibly to die with enough exposure. Red kryptonite causes him to act bizarrely. Blue kryptonite removes Superman's superpowers. Black kryptonite can split Superman's personality. Silver kryptonite causes paranoid delusions, and so on. Green Lantern has a vulnerability to the color yellow, or to wood, depending on which version of the superhero one prefers. J'onn J'onzz, Manhunter from Mars, is vulnerable to flame. Wonder Woman is perhaps just too nice and at times lets enemies take advantage of her. Yet all of the superheroes manage to fight for good and combat evil. They illustrate an important point about life: No matter how good someone is, that someone is likely to have a vulnerability that enemies will try to exploit.

All of us, like the superheroes, have our weaknesses and sometimes our superweaknesses. When successful leaders are brought down, it is often because they have a vulnerability that they fail adequately to acknowledge or to reckon with. Leaders like Bill Clinton, Eliot Spitzer, and Newt Gingrich come to mind. All had levels of success that were reduced because of their failure to confront a weakness. The superheroes of the comic books have the enormous advantage that they understand their weaknesses, or at least, their physical ones. Many of us lack such understanding.

In psychology, a popular theory is the theory of general intelligence, according to which people are mentally good at most things or bad at most things. The theory of general intelligence is a weakness in the field of psychology. Those who do well by it—who score high on standardized tests of abilities—may be blindsided because of their failure to realize that their creative, practical, wisdom-based, or emotional-intellectual skills may not match their IQs. Superman was able to survive, despite his vulnerability to kryptonite, only because he was aware of this vulnerability and thus able to take precautions against it. Standardized tests need to move away from merely global measures—an overall ACT score, a combined SAT score—because such composite scores hide patterns both of strength and of weakness. People are best able to succeed when they know their strengths and are able to capitalize on them and also know the internal vulnerabilities they bring to a situation and how they can control those vulnerabilities.

Two recent US presidents illustrate the point. George W. Bush characterized himself as "the decider." He has even named his autobiography of his presidency *Decision Points*. But from all indications, he was not a reflective thinker and, true to the image of himself he promoted as president, tended to shoot from the hip. This tendency caused problems on multiple occasions, such as his decision to enter into a war with Iraq based on reports of weapons of mass destruction that were in fact false. More recently, Barack Obama proved to be a brilliant campaigner but, by most accounts, a somewhat less effective president in his first term. On health care, he left it to Congress to work out the details of the health care bill and other initiatives. His lack of a clear vision of where he was leading the country—in Don't Ask, Don't Tell, in health care, in combating unemployment—contributed to the undoing of many candidates running for office in the off-year elections of 2010. One could criticize either of these individuals, but the point is not that they have weaknesses but rather that we all do. Like the superheroes, we fare much better when we understand what those weaknesses are. Some of these weaknesses stem from sketchy childhoods.

Superheroes did not necessarily have great childhoods. Superman was separated from his birth parents and brought up in a foster home by Jonathan and Martha Kent. Batman's parents were killed when he is a youth as he looks on. These catastrophes no doubt had profound effects on the superheroes, and in the movie series, Batman is constantly battling the effects of the psychic scars of his early childhood.

For all their weaknesses, superheroes excel in making up for sketchy childhoods. We can all learn from them in that regard. In a society that relishes stories of victimhood, it is perhaps not surprising that often, when a criminal is tried for repugnant behavior, the criminal's unfortunate childhood is brought into evidence by the defense attorneys. About the time I am writing these words, Steven J. Hayes has been sentenced to death for his part in the gruesome murder case that resulted from a home invasion against a doctor and his family in Cheshire, Connecticut. The unfortunate-childhood argument is weakened by the obvious lack of a control group: The lawyers for the perpetrators of crimes never mention all the people with unfortunate childhoods who did not become criminals.

Although few superheroes have criminal tendencies, they are sometimes treated like criminals. At the very least, many superheroes find themselves, at one point or another, in the disfavor of the general public. Spider-Man, for example, was at times viewed as a menace. The Shadow aroused the suspicions of the police. They fought for justice even when they were in public disfavor.

The superheroes are willing to defy the crowd, when need be, to do the right thing. They are not merely smart, therefore, but also creative. Creative individuals are those who are willing to defy the crowd—to do the opposite of what legions of people may expect and even demand they do. This willingness to defy the crowd in the name of right is part of what marks them as superheroes. They are ethical despite the costs.

The superheroes have in common that they seek a common good and that they behave ethically. Do the supervillains have anything in common? It turns out that they do. One can learn as much from the supervillains as from the superheroes because they exemplify the characteristics with which young (or old) people should disidentify. So if one looks at Lex Luthor, or the Joker, the Green Goblin, or Dr. Doom, or any of the supervillains in the James Bond series, one finds certain common characteristics:

- *Massive egocentrism.* They believe they are the center of the universe and literally try to place themselves at the center of the human universe. They see others as tools to serve them.
- *Lack of conscience.* They really do not care what happens to other people so long as their ego needs are met. If anything, they enjoy seeing others suffer, especially the superheroes.
- *Exploitativeness.* They exploit people shamelessly to their own ends. They have no qualms about using other people for their self-glorification and in the service of executing their plans.
- *Unrealistic optimism.* They are quite convinced their diabolical plots will succeed. It is this unrealistic optimism that often brings them down as the superheroes take advantage of it to defeat the supervillains.

- *False omniscience.* They believe they are either all-knowing or so hugely knowledgeable that there is little they can learn from anyone else. They often fail to learn from experience, which can further lead to their doom.
- *False invulnerability.* They think they are all-powerful, failing to recognize their own weaknesses.
- *False omnipotence.* They believe they are, or at least should be, all-powerful.
- *Ethical disengagement.* They leave ethics to others; they have little or no sense of ethics of their own.

Interestingly, supervillains seem to have one thing in common with superheroes, which is their immortality. In the end the superhero can defeat them, but, typically, only temporarily. They almost always come back. In a sense, the whole enterprise of the superhero comics represents a kind of Manichaeist view of the world in which good and evil exist forever, at odds with each other, with neither quite able to conquer the other. In a sense, in this worldview, neither group could exist without the other. The superheroes would have nothing to do without supervillains to fight, and moreover, their good is defined largely in terms of their opposition to the evil of the supervillains, just as the evil of the supervillains is defined largely in terms of their opposition to the good.

We all can learn a lot from superheroes. Perhaps what we can learn most of all is the value of wisdom and an ethical stance toward life. In the end, that is what the superheroes have in common, much more than any particular set of superpowers: They fight bad guys, sometimes against heavy odds and sometimes when onlookers are not even cheering the superheroes on. (This, of course, assumes that the superheroes do not view us, their readers and watchers, as onlookers!) Fighting for what is right and ethical would seem to be easy: Just do the right thing. But it is actually hard. Behaving ethically involves a number of steps. Unless an individual completes all these steps, he or she will not act ethically:

1. Recognize that there is an event to which to react

Superheroes seem to have a special ability to know when they are needed. If they are slow to react, they often have a "better half" who helps them see the need for their services, such as Margo Lane, friend of The Shadow. But we are not all so fortunate.

When people hear their political, educational, or especially religious leaders talk, they may not believe there is any reason to question what they hear. After all, they are listening to authority figures. In this way, leaders, including cynical and corrupt leaders, may lead their flocks to accept and even commit unethical acts, such as suicide bombings or murder of those whose beliefs diverge from one's own.

2. Define the event as having an ethical dimension

Superheroes are super in part because of their ability to recognize wrongness and injustice. Supervillains like Lex Luthor and real cynical leaders alike may flaunt their unethical behavior—one is reminded today of Robert Mugabe, but there are other world leaders who might equally be relevant here. When Mugabe and his henchmen seized the farms of white farmers, the seizure was presented as part of a plan to compensate alleged war heroes for their accomplishments. Why should it be unethical to compensate war heroes?

The Chinese government attempted to manipulate media to downplay the dimensions of an event with a huge ethical component. On May 12, 2008, an earthquake in Sichuan province killed an estimated ten thousand schoolchildren. But there was an irregularity in the buildings that imploded during the earthquake. Schools for children of well-connected party leaders, as well as government buildings, withstood the earthquake with no problem. In contrast, schools housing poor children crumbled to dust. It turned out that the schools had been built in ways that could only poorly withstand an earthquake. Presumably, the money that was supposed to have supported better construction went to line the pockets of Party functionaries.

3. Decide that the ethical dimension is significant

A superhero has to decide whether a case is significant enough for him or her to take on. The superhero can't solve every problem of villainy in the world. In real life as in the comics, some leaders seem to specialize in trying to downplay the ethical dimension of their behavior. One was Bill Clinton, in his behavior with Monica Lewinsky and his subsequent concealment of it. Eliot Spitzer later followed a similar route, leading to his resignation as governor of New York. Mark Sanford also had some unfortunate romantic entanglements but chose not to resign as governor of South Carolina. It is not only politicians: people who behave unethically, whether supervillains or ordinary humans, often see not themselves but their unappreciative audience as the problem.

4. Take responsibility for generating an ethical solution to the problem

Supervillains never take responsibility for the evil they perpetrate on the world. People may allow leaders to commit wretched acts because they figure it is the leaders' responsibility to determine the ethical dimensions of their actions. Isn't that why they are leaders in the first place? Or people may assume that the leaders, especially if they are religious leaders, are in a uniquely good position to determine what is ethical. If a religious leader encourages someone to become a suicide bomber, that "someone" may feel that being such a bomber must be ethical. Why else would a religious leader suggest it?

5. Figure out what abstract ethical rule(s) might apply to the problem

Superheroes need to ask themselves, if they feel an act is unethical, what makes it so? Otherwise, they risk punishing the wrong people. People who act unethically often go to great lengths to obfuscate exactly what they did, making it hard to know what rule to apply to the situation because it is not even clear what the situation is.

6. Decide how these abstract ethical rules actually apply to the problem so as to suggest a concrete solution

Superheroes need to decide what action is ethically appropriate: Do they kill villains, otherwise punish them, turn them over to the authorities, let them go? If one follows reports in the media, there are any number of instances in which pastors who are highly trained in religion and ethics act in unethical and unscrupulous ways—Ted Haggard, Jimmy Swaggert, and Jim Bakker come to mind. They may be able to teach classes on ethics, but they fail to translate what they teach into their own behavior.

7. Prepare for counteracting contextual forces that might lead one not to act in an ethical manner

As mentioned above, superheroes often get little environmental support for doing the right thing. Sometimes even the legal authorities resist. In real life, the problem often is not that other people seem oblivious to the ethical implications of the situation, but that they actively encourage you to behave in ways you define as unethical. In the Rwandan genocides, Hutus were encouraged to hate Tutsis and to kill them, even if they were within their own family. Those who were not willing to participate in the massacres risked becoming victims themselves. The same applied in Hitler's Germany. Those who tried to save Jews from concentration camps themselves risked going to such camps.

In genocides, opposing the perpetrators may make one a victim. Or one may look foolish acting in an ethical way when others are taking advantage of a situation in a way to foster their personal good. Even before one acts, one may be hesitant because of the aftermath one anticipates, whether real or merely imagined.

We would like to think that the pressure to behave ethically will lead people to resist internal temptations to act poorly. But often, exactly the opposite is the case. In the Enron case, when Sherron Watkins blew the whistle on unethical behavior, she was punished and made to feel like an "outcast." In general, whistleblowers are treated poorly, despite the protections they are supposed to receive.

8. Act

Superheroes sometimes hesitate to act, but in the end, they almost always do the right thing. Ordinary people don't. They often get all the way up to Step 8, and then simply fail to act, perhaps because they fear the repercussions.

We can learn a lot from superheroes. Most of all, we can learn that when things are not as they should be, we have a choice, difficult though it may be. We can act if only we choose to.

TEN

Seven Roads to Justice for Superheroes and Humans

Mikhail Lyubansky

EDITOR'S NOTE

Some superheroes are official or unofficial arms of law enforcement: They apprehend criminals who then are processed by police and enter the criminal justice system. Other superheroes are basically vigilantes. Superheroes dispense—and have the power to dispense—a variety of types of justice. Mikhail Lyubansky uses his knowledge of group relations, identity, and restorative justice to classify the different types of justice systems within which superheroes operate and proposes a new type of justice dispensed by a new type of superhero.

—Robin S. Rosenberg

I like superheroes. I think I always have. Like many kids, I grew up reading the comics, and when I bumped into Alan Moore's *Watchmen* as a college freshman in 1989, I thought I had discovered the greatest novel ever written. I'm still not entirely sure that it isn't.

As a child, I was drawn in by the characters' superpowers and the imaginative story arcs, but superhero stories are not just juvenile entertainment. Like speculative fiction in general, superhero stories are ultimately a window into humanity. The fictional universes allow the writers to manipulate the circumstances to better examine the most complex aspects of the human experience, none more so than the issues of morality and justice.

Though they might be physically or intellectually superior to ordinary humans, superheroes generally operate within the same kind of justice systems as those of us living in what we call "the real world." Thus, looking at superhero justice allows us to better understand our own justice system and consider the various ways in which it does and doesn't meet both society's and our own needs. I will start with the question of punishment, a response to justice that is very much at the heart of contemporary critiques of real-world justice systems.

VENGEFUL JUSTICE

As in our own justice system, superhero justice is mostly synonymous with punishment. Most superheroes do not literally follow the biblical edict of "an eye for an eye,"[1] but they do tend to share our own cultural belief that "the punishment must fit the crime."

Though different heroes do have somewhat different moral codes, almost all tend to endorse a punitive response, either explicitly or implicitly. At the most punitive end are antiheroes like Rorschach (Watchmen) and the aptly named Punisher, who first appeared in *The Amazing Spider-Man #129*.

Like Lisbeth Salander, the diminutive heroine of *The Girl with the Dragon Tattoo*, the Punisher works outside the formal (and legal) justice system, unrestricted by its bureaucracy, unencumbered by its corruption, unfettered by the safeguards that were designed to protect the innocent but sometimes end up protecting the guilty too. With the Punisher, guilt is rarely questioned by either the protagonist or the audience. We know beyond a reasonable doubt that the offender is guilty, and the Punisher is not much concerned with the complexity of either the criminal mind or the criminal act. Motivations for the act don't matter either, because the prevailing assumption is that the offender in question is a "bad seed" that cannot be rehabilitated. Indeed, one does not rehabilitate monsters; one kills them. And there is no greater hero than that of the monster slayer who not only protects the rest of us from evil but takes vengeance against it. We celebrate the Punisher for his willingness to exact such vengeance, not in spite of his willingness to employ murder, kidnapping, extortion, and torture, but because of it.

Rooting for the Punisher is relatively easy, especially if one accepts the notion of unredeemable evil. The appeal of Rorschach is more complicated. In *The Gospel According to Superheroes*,[2] B. J. Oropeza describes what may be the character's defining scene in the novel:

> In one flashback scene, he discovers the remains of a kidnapped child whose bones are being devoured by German shepherds. He kills the dogs with an ax, and after immobilizing the kidnapper with a handcuff, he lights the criminal's place on fire, giving the man a hacksaw with the option to either saw off his wrist with his free hand or be burned alive in the house.

"In short," Oropeza concludes, "Rorschach is not a well person." (p. 201)

He wasn't intended to be. *Watchmen* was intended as a commentary on a variety of approaches to justice, with the different costumed heroes each representing a specific philosophical perspective. Rorschach, the lone-wolf vigilante, is undeniably appealing on many levels, most notably his courage, resolve, and creative problem-solving, which are essential because, like Batman, he doesn't have real superpowers. However, he is also shown to have a limited ability to process complexity. In Rorschach's eyes (as in the Punisher's), an act is either right or wrong. There is no in-between. And if the act is wrong, then justice must be done in the form of immediate "eye for an eye" retribution. No other strategy is acceptable. No other response is possible.

The appeal of Rorschach might well lie in how he equates justice with vengeance. We might disagree with him about who is right and wrong, perhaps even about who is innocent and who is guilty. But most readers can be sure to agree on one thing: Those who are guilty (heroes included) of vile crimes need to pay, and we admire Rorschach for his uncompromising willingness to exact vengeance regardless of circumstances or even the law itself.

That last part is crucial. Our formal justice systems also exact vengeance—capital punishment can certainly be viewed in this way—but they do so in a more systematic way (i.e., due process) and with the full support of the government and its people.

PUNITIVE JUSTICE

Our real justice system is not nearly as rigid as Rorschach's. It can take into consideration "extenuating circumstances" and, rather than relying on the moral code of a single self-appointed vigilante, it consists of numerous highly trained professionals who are granted authority by the State to apprehend, judge, and, if necessary, punish the identified offender. At the same time, there is little doubt that the real-world criminal justice systems are primarily punitive[3] in nature, as typically are the school and work justice systems that are usually in place to deal with conflict and rule violations.

These punitive systems are so widespread that most of us have a hard time even imagining any alternative ways of "doing" justice. The superheroes don't help in this regard. Many of our most recognizable costumed crime-fighters, including DC's Superman, Batman, and the Flash, and Marvel's Fantastic Four and Avengers (who include dozens of rotating heroes, most notably Iron Man, Thor, and Captain America) are similarly punitive in their approach. They communicate with government representatives, police, and other formal authority figures and almost always turn the criminals over to those same authorities. The superheroes are typically allies to the police and other parts of the criminal justice system in the fight against crime and frequently work within the same system.

To be sure, there are times when superheroes question the justice systems they supposedly serve, and it is precisely such exceptions that provide meaningful commentary on our own justice systems. Marvel's Civil War storyline serves as a good example. This story arc takes place on the heels of the tragedy in Stamford, Connecticut, when a group of young superheroes were unable to prevent the supervillain Nitro from killing 612 civilians. In the aftermath, Tony Stark (Iron Man) wants every superhero to register with the government and novice heroes to be properly trained in order to avoid both a repeat of Stamford and the possibility of a harsh government response that might outlaw costumed crime-fighting entirely (this incidentally is the backdrop in *Watchmen*). Stark argues that heroes should be properly trained, not left to their own devices, and held accountable to the public and the legal system, in the same way police officers are accountable. Captain America, on the other hand, believes that such registration would place family members and friends of superheroes at almost certain risk; he heads the resistance. The other superheroes (and villains) line up on one side or the other in a memorable story line that also doubled as an allegorical commentary on 9/11 and the Patriot Act. As plot lines go, the Civil War is compelling, both for the thrill of seeing Iron Man and Captain America on opposing sides, as well as (for more mature readers) the ethical undertones of the allegorical commentary.

Yet, even as they disagree about politics (i.e., the Superhero Registration Act), Iron Man and Captain America never actually disagree on what justice ought to look like. Both seek to apprehend criminals and turn them over to the authorities. Indeed, Captain America and his group of secret Avengers (which includes the Punisher, Storm, and Black Panther) continue to fight crime, capturing and tying up criminals for the benefit of authority, even as they themselves try to evade the government's (and Iron Man's) efforts to find and bring them to justice.

REHABILITORY JUSTICE

It is worth noting here that most superhero stories end with the villain's capture. Though there are exceptions to the rule, for the most part what happens after the villain is apprehended is rarely depicted. Rather, the presence of police officers or other easily recognized authority figures is intended to imply that the formal justice system would take it from there. More specifically, the handing over of the villain to the formal authority implies that there will be a trial to determine guilt (we already know they're not innocent from the story arc), followed by incarceration or other type of restricted confinement necessitated by the villain's superpowers.

But is this type of formal punishment always in society's best interest? The comics occasionally suggest an alternative, as when Harvey Dent (Two Face) winds up in a hospital, under psychiatric care, rather than in a prison. Dent is a former district attorney of Gotham City, who often appears as Batman's nemesis. While the origin of his "Dr. Jeckyl and Mr. Hyde" persona has seen multiple incarnations, his evildoing is most frequently shown to be a result of either psychosis (voices telling him to do evil things) or dissociative identity disorder (a fragmenting of a personality into distinct alters such that each has a mind of his/her own). As a result, Dent often winds up in some kind of psychiatric treatment facility rather than a prison.

As it happens, the psychiatric treatment Dent typically receives is not only substandard but unethical. In *The Dark Knight Returns*,[4] Dr. Bartholomew Wolper, who is the psychiatrist of both Dent and the Joker, believes that his patients are the victims of Batman's psychological issues:

> You see, it all gets down to this Batman fellow. Batman's psychotic sublimative/psycho erotic behavior pattern is like a net. Weak-egoed neurotics, like Harvey, are drawn into corresponding intersticing patterns. You might say Batman commits the crimes...using his so-called villains as narcissistic proxies. (p. 47)

Not only does Wolper blame Batman for his patients' criminal behavior, he actively campaigns for his capture (and the Joker's release). Thus, psychiatry, and by extension the entire mental health system, is set up as a foil for our superhero and for justice, more broadly.

Even when psychiatrists are not portrayed to be immoral and corrupt, they are still emasculated and ridiculed for being unable to do their job. We see this, for example, in *Watchmen*, when Rorschach is interviewed by prison psychiatrist Dr. Malcolm Long. Unlike Wolper, Long is neither unethical nor corrupt. Rather, when he first meets Rorschach, he is content with his life, optimistic, and well-meaning. Long believes he can rehabilitate Rorschach and maybe learn about the vigilante mind in the process. Rorschach initially taunts him and effortlessly circumvents the psychiatric assessment (the Rorschach Test, what else?) but eventually shares his real dark history. Unfortunately, Rorschach's forthcoming results neither in his healing nor in Long gaining clinical insight into vigilantism. Rather, Long gradually becomes so obsessed and personally impacted, that his own contentment and happy marriage are both shattered. By the end of their time together, it is Long who is looking at the ink blots and seeing nothing but darkness:

> I looked at the Rorschach blot. I tried to pretend it looked like a spreading tree, shadows pooled beneath it, but it didn't. It looked more like a dead cat I once found, the fat, glistening grubs writhing blindly, squirming over each other, frantically tunneling away from the light. But even that is avoiding the real horror. The horror is this: In the end, it is simply a picture of empty meaningless blackness. We are alone. There is nothing else. (VI.28.4)

During their time together, Rorschach clearly has little respect for Long, accusing him of being fat (and, by extension lazy), not understanding pain, and seeking professional prestige under the guise of "treatment." In a different comic, this critique might reasonably be interpreted as character-specific, but *Watchmen* is not just another comic. It is a sharp commentary on both society and the comic industry itself. In the words of writer Alan Moore, the intention was to create "a superhero Moby Dick, something that had that sort of weight, that sort of density."[5] Thus, Rorschach's indictment of Long may reasonably be read as an indictment of psychiatry and mental health, more generally.

Altogether, superhero comics suggest that, at best, mental health professionals have no useful understanding of people or their motivations and, at worst, are morally corrupt and willing to use their authority to obfuscate justice. Rather than being a viable alternative to the criminal justice system, the mental health system is portrayed as incompetent, unethical, and in all ways undesirable as a response to criminal behavior, which, of course, invalidates the concept of rehabilitative justice and serves to support and maintain the reliance on punitive practices.

The indictment of the mental health system is unfair (especially in terms of ethics) but not entirely without merit. Psychologists have struggled to separate the concept of psychopathy from criminal behavior. Psychopathy is a condition presumed to be characterized by a variety of personality traits, most notably a lack of empathy or remorse, but also emotional manipulation, impulsivity, aggression, and a lack of response to punishment. However, these characteristics have proven to be extremely difficult to measure and, despite considerable efforts by many professionals, at this point "there is no consensus about the symptom criteria for psychopathy, and no psychiatric or psychological organization has sanctioned a diagnosis of 'psychopathy' itself."[6] Not surprisingly, then, the current version of the *Diagnostic and Statistical Manual of Mental Disorders* avoids psychopathy and includes instead diagnostic criteria for antisocial personality disorder (ASPD), which focuses on behavior patterns rather than personality characteristics. The ASPD diagnosis has little utility, however, as it may not adequately identify those who would benefit from mental health treatment from those convicted of crimes (a 2002 review of studies showed that 47 percent of male prisoners had ASPD).[7] Moreover, even if correctly identified, there is presently no empirically validated treatment for either ASPD or psychopathy. In short, there is, as yet, no suitable mental health alternative for criminals like the Joker, Green Goblin, and many others, who are clearly suffering from psychopathy, just as there are, as yet, no suitable mental health alternatives for real-world serial-killers.

The vast majority of criminals, however, are not psychopaths, and even the much broader ASPD diagnosis excludes the majority of those convicted of a crime. These kinds of criminals—the ones who have committed murder in a moment of passionate rage or those who turn to drug trafficking because it is the only survival path they see—are rarely depicted in the superhero universe because they aren't compelling foils for the superpowered heroes. However, they comprise the vast majority of the prison population. Many of these "regular" criminals suffer from a variety of mental health issues, including depression, post-traumatic stress disorder (PTSD), substance dependence, and occasionally, psychotic disorders, like schizophrenia. Unlike psychopathy, effective treatment options exist for all of the above, and it certainly seems worth asking if our society might be better off treating some criminals instead of punishing them, or at least doing both.

METAPHYSICAL JUSTICE

Of all the costumed heroes in *Watchmen*, only one, physicist Jon Osterman (Dr. Manhattan), has actual superpowers, thanks to an accident in which he was disintegrated into atoms in an intrinsic field subtractor and somehow able to reconstruct a physical body. Osterman's powers include superhuman strength, telekinesis, teleportation, control over matter at a subatomic level, and, most importantly for this discussion, almost total clairvoyance—the ability to see the past, present, and future everywhere simultaneously. What does justice look like from this kind of godlike perspective? It's hard for humans to even imagine, but *Watchmen* gamely tries.

We first see Osterman's unusual orientation toward human life when Rorschach informs him of the Comedian's death and warns him that other costumed crime fighters may also be in danger.

> A live body and a dead body contain the same number of particles. Structurally, there's no discernible difference. Life and death are unquantifiable abstracts. Why should I be concerned? (I.23.3)

As the story unfolds, we learn that, despite his omniscience (or perhaps because of it), Osterman espouses a philosophy of predestination. "Everything is preordained. Even my responses," he tells his former girlfriend Laurie Juspeczyk, during their long talk on Mars, adding, "We're all puppets, Laurie. I'm just a puppet who can see the strings."

Although he clearly altered the course of the Vietnam War (shown in flashback), in "real-time" Osterman declines to interfere in either interpersonal conflicts (as when the Comedian kills the enraged Vietnamese woman he had apparently impregnated) or international ones, intimating that he cannot interfere because his own actions (and presumably lack of actions) are already predetermined. As Osterman sees it, he cannot interfere with the unfolding of events because they've already happened.

> There is no future. There is no past. Do you see? Time is simultaneous, an intricately structured jewel that humans insist on viewing one edge at a time, when the whole design is visible in every facet. (IX.6.5–6)

What, then, is justice when everything has happened, is happening, will happen at the same time? Are we to believe that from the perspective of an all-knowing and all-powerful being, there is no meaningful distinction between injustice and justice, no required action to transform the former into the latter?

Osterman's words to Adrian Veidt (also known as Ozymandias), near the end of the novel, suggest this may be the case.

> I have walked across the surface of the sun. I have witnessed events so tiny and so fast, they could hardly be said to have occurred at all. But you, Adrian, you're just a man. The world's smartest man poses no more threat to me than does its smartest termite. (XII.18.3–4)

Osterman is explaining to Veidt why it was such folly for Veidt to attempt to kill him, but there is a deeper meaning in this passage. To Osterman, human beings and their conflicts are not distinguishable from termites, a species perhaps worthy of observation but one so far below our level of consciousness that it would not occur to even the most moral among us to attempt to adjudicate or otherwise interfere in their conflicts as an ethical imperative.

Yet, Osterman ultimately backs away from his philosophy of noninterference. His conversation on Mars with Laurie reawakens his interest in humanity.

> The world is so full of people, so crowded with these miracles that they become commonplace and we forget…I forget. We gaze continually at the world and it grows dull in our perceptions. Yet seen from another's vantage point, as if new, it may still take our breath away. Come…dry your eyes, for you are life, rarer than a quark and unpredictable beyond the dreams of Heisenberg. Come, dry your eyes. And let's go home. (IX.27.3–28.2)

It seems like a happy moment: Osterman realizes the beauty and value of humanity and commits himself to saving it. But it's worth noting what it is that changes Osterman's mind. It is not Juspeczyk's pleas that sway Osterman, but her realization and willingness to come to terms with the fact that her biological father was none other than the Comedian, Edward Blake, who once attempted to rape her mother but became her father as a result of a later, consensual relationship. It is not humanity's potential for goodness that sways Osterman but what he refers to as the thermodynamic miracle of each life-form emerging from the complexity and unpredictability of human emotions and behaviors.

Though not explicit, Osterman's observations about perspective and his new insight into the complexity of human behavior both have implications for real-world justice. What may seem like an obvious injustice from close range (e.g., a person smashing a car with a crowbar) may have very different meaning with the benefit of distance (the owner of the car had refused to transport the crowbar wielder's mother to the hospital and the mother did not survive the night). What would be just in such a case? To arrest the man with the crowbar? To charge the car owner with manslaughter? What if we zoomed further out still and learned that the man who owned the car refused the hospital trip because he worked for a drug gang that was planning to use the car for business that same night? What if the drug gang's activities actually funded the nearby hospital, as well as other local services because the official government did not have a presence in the community, as in many Brazilian favelas? What should justice look like, then? From a metaphysical perspective, it depends entirely on the level of analysis. This seems like something worth keeping in mind, even if only as a reminder to remain humble and recognize the humanity of those whom we see as having acted against society.

STRUCTURAL JUSTICE

Sometimes, evil is not so much an individual phenomenon as a cultural one. Many of our favorite superheroes, including Captain America and Wonder Woman, were originally created to do battle with the Nazis. Despite the presence of Red Skull, justice in those early stories was not so much about apprehending a particular nemesis as fighting the Nazi menace. Notably, the cover of the first issue of Captain America, which went on sale in December 1940, showed Cap punching Adolf Hitler in the jaw.

More recently, superhero comics have taken on the cold war (*Watchmen*) and a variety of social issues, including racism, poverty, substance abuse, and the government's willingness to use violence to achieve its aims. In the December 2001 issue of *The Amazing Spider-Man*, Spider-Man, Captain America, and Daredevil assist in the clean-up after the 9/11 attack and lament their inability to see it coming and do something to prevent it. This brief story arc, which positioned the firefighters and human clean-up crew as the "real heroes," went along with the prevailing spirit of patriotism that swept across the United States in the months following the attack. However it is not unusual for comics to take a critical perspective on U.S. policy and systemic structures. In *Marvel Boy* #5, for example, Noh-Varr (aka Marvel Boy, Captain Marvel, The Protector), a member of the alien Kree race who has decidedly mixed feelings toward Earth, explains his dissatisfaction:

> There *is* no system here. There's nothing but fear and greed and stupidity. As far as I can see the planet is run by primitive primeurban *protection rackets* with something called *"Law"* as the only thing dividing *one* gang's methods from another. Your leaders are *murderers* who say violence is *wrong*, then drop bombs whenever they have a point to make. *Millions* of your people can't even get shelter or enough to *eat*. [emphases in original]

Noh-Varr is speaking about a fictional Earth (Earth-616), but this context is allegorical. His words are as much about the United States and its government as about the fictional universe in which he lives. In the fictional universe, Noh-Varr goes on to battle against Doctor Midas, a greedy, power-hungry scientist who eventually becomes the evil Cosmic Man, and a sentient corporation named Hexus, which had aims to consume all rivals and become the most powerful entity in the universe. On an allegorical level, the *Marvel Boy* plot line is a scathing critique of real-world U.S. policy and corporate greed.

Probably the most recognizable attempt to promote structural justice in the superhero universe has been the ongoing story of the X-Men, a group of humans who, as a result of some genetic mutation in the X-gene, developed some form of superhuman ability and, as a result, became something different than human. The X-Men wear costumes and fight "bad guys," but at their soul the franchise has always been less about superpowers and more about human tendencies to fear and hate those who are different and the various ways we deal with such tendencies. As long-time X-Men writer Chris Claremont (1982) put it, "what we have here, intended or not, is a book that is about racism, bigotry and prejudice."

The remark about "intentionality" is noteworthy. It's quite possible that prejudice was far from the minds of writer Stan Lee and illustrator Jack Kirby, when they first introduced the X-Men in 1963. At the very least, given that the original ensemble of X-Men was entirely racially and ethnically homogeneous (as per the comic industry's standard of the time), the themes of prejudice were most likely not very well thought out at first. Nonetheless, the seeds of these themes were planted in the very first issue when Charles Xavier, a mutant telepath responsible for training and organizing the mutants into the X-Men, observed that human beings are not yet ready to accept superpowered individuals in their midst (*X-Men #1*). By 1975 the X-Men were ethnically and racially diverse, featuring Canadian (Wolverine), Russian (Colossus), German (Nightcrawler), and African (Storm) characters that reflected the comic's ideology of tolerance and multiculturalism[8]—an ideology that was a good decade ahead of its time.

Before long, the X-Men story lines clearly encouraged readers to see the mutants as an allegory for oppression in general and to generalize Professor Xavier's philosophy of tolerance and assimilation to other oppressed groups, including racial and ethnic minorities.

The question of race is especially pertinent to issues of justice, because though our own justice systems are supposed to be unbiased, the data show consistent racial bias in seemingly every aspect of our criminal justice system.

Consider some recent racial profiling data from my home state of Illinois, where the Illinois Department of Transportation (IDOT) has been compiling racial profiling data for almost 10 years. According to the 2009 data (the most recent available at the time of this writing), "minority drivers" were 12 percent more likely to be stopped (after controlling for demographic differences in population) and more than twice as likely to have their car searched (this requires consent, but consent is given nearly 90 percent of the time).

When confronted with such data, police officers (and chiefs) usually respond that they are merely doing their job—that the racial discrepancy in stops and searches merely reflects group differences in criminal behavior. Yet, the city's own data suggest otherwise. Those consensual searches? They yielded contraband (either weapons or drugs) for 16 percent of the "minority drivers" compared to almost 24 percent of "Caucasian drivers" (see bottom row in Table 10.1[9] below).

These numbers are not an aberration. They are exactly at the state's 6-year average (15% vs. 24%). If there were true probable cause, the percentages would be roughly the same.

Unfortunately, this is not just a policing issue. Similar bias is evident in the U.S. incarceration rates, where the racial disparities are so high that, in the words of attorney and writer Michelle

Table 10.1. Illinois Traffic Stop Study, 2009. Agency: Illinois Statewide.

Stops				
	Caucasian Drivers		**Minority Drivers**	
Total Stops	1,672,913		796,491	
Percentage Stops	68		32	
Duration (Mean\Median)	12\10		14\10	
Estimated Minority Driving Population			28.48	
Ratio			1.12	
Reason for Stop				
	Caucasian Drivers		**Minority Drivers**	
Total	1,672,877		796,202	
Moving Violations	1,228,815	73%	529,101	66%
Equipment Violations	308,762	18%	177,588	22%
Licensing / Registration Violations	135,257	8%	89,215	11%
Outcome for Stop				
	Caucasian Drivers		**Minority Drivers**	
Total	1,672,913		796,491	
Citation	930,829	56%	499,378	63%
Written Warning	507,380	30%	164,058	21%
Verbal Warning/Stop Card	234,704	14%	133,055	17%
Consent Searches				
	Caucasian Drivers		**Minority Drivers**	
Total	1,672,913		796,491	
Requested	13,625	1%	12,618	2%
Granted	11,558	85%	11,368	90%
Performed	11,112	96%	10,974	97%
Found	2,677	24%	1,721	16%

Alexander, "the racial dimension of incarceration is its most striking feature."[10]

Superheroes don't generally examine their own racial profiling tendencies, and I have seen no published studies examining race-group differences in the incarceration rates of those convicted of a crime in the superhero universe. Even so, the X-Men franchise does have something worthwhile to say about real-world racism. While *X-Men* does not address racism directly, the franchise does more than merely model an ideology of tolerance and diversity. It examines the causes of prejudice and intolerance and pits competing perspectives against each other as different characters try to come to terms with the ethical and psychological implications brought on by the dawn of a new evolutionary phase in which mutants and humans struggle to coexist.

The racial metaphors in the superhero comics have often been flawed and problematic, as for example, when the often villainous Magneto tells Xavier, "The [human-mutant] war is coming, and I intend to fight it by any means necessary."[11] However, unlike news coverage of crime (as well as most other fictional stories about justice), the X-Men franchise placed prejudice front and center, exactly where it needs to be, given the racial discrepancies that pervade our police blotters and prisons. To be sure, the X-Men were exceptional in this respect, but at least they serve as an exemplar for both those of us interested in justice and comic fans more broadly.

RESTORATIVE JUSTICE

If superhero comics can sometimes present a vision of justice for the real world to follow, the industry has also been surprisingly conservative in its support and glorification of retributive models of justice. This is nowhere more evident than in the absence of not only restorative superheroes but restorative practices more generally.[12]

Restorative practices have been around for thousands of years and are part of the traditions of indigenous people all over the world. Unlike punitive and retributive notions of justice, restorative approaches focus on identifying and "restoring" the harm that was done rather than on punishing the person who is determined to have caused the harm. In restorative practices, the goals are truth-telling (and listening), responsibility taking, and voluntary agreements about how to go forward.

Occasional social issue story aside, the emphasis on punitive justice in the superhero universe is not coincidental. The 1954 Comics Code which, at the time, had to be followed in order to have the right to sell comics, had all of the following statutes:

- Crimes shall never be presented in such a way as to create sympathy for the criminal, to promote distrust of the forces of law and justice, or to inspire others with a desire to imitate criminals.
- If crime is depicted it shall be as a sordid and unpleasant activity.
- Criminals shall not be presented so as to be rendered glamorous or to occupy a position which creates a desire for emulation.
- In every instance good shall triumph over evil and the criminal punished for his misdeeds.

In other words, restorative practices were literally outlawed in the superhero universe.

The Comics Code underwent significant revisions in the 1980s and 1990s and was abandoned altogether in the 2000s, but for some reason, restorative superheroes—that is, superheroes who espouse a clear restorative worldview, never came. In some ways, this is not surprising. Restorative practices often require community members to hold each other accountable and work together to repair the harm rather than rely on some authority to do it. As such, restorative superheroes are, in a way, an oxymoron because they, by definition, are superior to others and, therefore, usually take on the duties of taking care of other people's conflicts. In the words of Peter Parker's Uncle Ben, "With great power there must also come—great responsibility."[13]

For Spider-Man and other superheroes, Uncle Ben's words (originally attributed to Voltaire), provide a necessary moral grounding, but what do they imply for those of us who lack great powers? In my reading, they suggest that those of us with little structural (or personal) power have little or no responsibility to respond to injustice and conflict. Our justice systems support this view, as well.

Our formal justice systems (including those in the schools and workplaces) typically professionalize the handling of conflict. They identify individuals who are authorized to decide who is right and wrong and what needs to happen next. There are benefits of such an approach, but there are costs too, and one of these is that those directly involved in the conflict and those who are most affected by it do not typically take the responsibility for working things out. Restorative practices tend to put the responsibility back in the hands of those who are actually part of the conflict, not in some supposedly objective, well-trained (or super) outsider.[14]

That said, there is still room, I think, for a restorative superhero.

We can see features of restorative principles in several existing superheroes. Aquaman's most recognizable power, for example, is essentially enhanced communication skills—in his case with the marine community, which he summons when he needs help, and it is notable that Wonder Woman's greatest weapon against crime is truth, in the form of her magic lasso. Yet, both Aquaman and Wonder Woman also work within the conventional punitive systems, apprehending the criminals and turning them over to the authorities as members of the Justice League. Wonder Woman, in particular, essentially functions as a superpowered detective, one who combines the threat of physical harm with an interrogation technique (her lasso) that is efficient at getting the truth. But these truths are not offered voluntarily, and the marine life that comes to Aquaman's aid does so in order to overpower his adversaries. Neither is intended to have a restorative effect and neither produces one.

A truly restorative superhero does not yet exist, but that doesn't mean one could not be created. I can imagine such a hero. Let's call her Empathy. She would be human, with no extraordinary physical powers but an unusually well developed ability to feel compassion, not only for those who are harmed but for those who perpetrate harm as well, including those who perpetrate evil. Along similar lines, Empathy is characterized by an inner peace and a capacity to recognize the needs of others and embrace everyone (even those who violently lash out against others) with empathy.

How would our hero walk in the world? How would she try to be restorative? It seems that this very question would be a necessary and ongoing part of Empathy's internal struggle. I can imagine Empathy trying a conventional approach—finding conflict and trying to work through it as some kind of supermediator before realizing that this was still another way of taking the responsibility for working through conflict out of the hands of those directly involved. An existential crisis might follow, leading Empathy to resign her hero status and responsibilities in order to lead Restorative Circles[15] and other restorative practices as a peer, rather than as an authority.

Of course, given her abilities, Empathy cannot, for long, continue her work on a small stage. After turning down multiple requests to facilitate conflict on a world scale, Empathy finally receives a request she is unable to refuse. With the fate of the world hanging in the balance, she reemerges into public life and creates the conditions for the world's governments to rehumanize each other and work together to restore peace. Though uncomfortable with what she regards as "undue credit"—it was the conflict parties themselves who resolved their differences, she insists—Empathy is left with a new purpose and decides to take on a new name: Mahametta.[16]

Eventually, Mahametta (who also becomes known as "the Facilitator") will find herself confronted by those, like the Punisher and Rorschach, who are driven by the need for vengeance. Might the Facilitator find a way to turn the Punisher away from his punitive methods? That story would be worth telling, because it would show that no one is beyond redemption. The Punisher might come to reevaluate his own childhood and the murder of his wife and kids that initially turned him into a punisher. Perhaps empathy and kindness from some unexpected source might lead him into self-empathy for the child who received the ultimate punishment, which might lead to empathy for violent criminals who, in some cases, may also be acting from a desire to punish those they perceived to have harmed them in some way.[17]

To be sure, the kind of transformation described above is hardly typical. More than likely, despite the Facilitator's best efforts, her words and actions will have little impact on the Punisher. Indeed, because restorative practices place a high premium on voluntariness, no outcome is ever assured. Sometimes, things just don't work out the way we hope, even in the comic books.

When we finally see a character like the Facilitator among the other superheroes, it will be a sure sign that restorative practices have fully infiltrated our society. In the meantime, restorative practices demand that we be our own superheroes, not in the sense of seeking vengeance but in the sense of being willing to walk toward conflict and engage with it ourselves, rather than relying on someone with actual super powers or an authority that is given super powers, like a judge. In this sense, there are already many superheroes among us. And room for many more.

ZEN JUSTICE

There is an old Zen story of an elderly farmer who had worked his crops for many years. One day his horse ran away. Upon hearing the news, his neighbors came to visit. "Such bad luck," they said sympathetically. "May be," the farmer replied. The next morning the horse returned, bringing with it three other wild horses. "How wonderful," the neighbors exclaimed. "May be," replied the old man. The following day, his son tried to ride one of the untamed horses, was thrown, and broke his leg. The neighbors again came to offer their sympathy on his misfortune. "May be," answered the farmer. The day after, military officials came to the village to draft young men into the army. Seeing that the son's leg was broken, they passed him by. The neighbors congratulated the farmer on how well things had turned out. "May be," said the farmer.

This story is usually used to caution readers from rushing to judgment.[18] One of its points is that it is not always immediately evident whether a particular event will have positive or negative consequences, even if it seems obvious (as it does in the examples above) that the consequences are clearly either good or bad. Indeed, because the story ends with yet another "may be," even a longer perspective is inadequate to judge any particular event, because something could happen the very next day that would turn everything on its head. Rather than judge, the story would have us accept things as they come, without judgment, and act accordingly.

It seems like good advice. And I have to admit that it's liberating to step into that nonjudgmental space. The wars in Iraq and Afghanistan? Maybe they will be a catalyst for a new era of world peace. The Occupy movement? Maybe it will lead to both economic and social reforms that raise the standard of living around the globe. Or, on the other hand, maybe it will wind up splintering the American people and ushering in decades of backlash against progressive politics and cultural tolerance.

The point is we just don't know. And we can't know. All we can do is just... be... and focus on accepting our circumstances, rather than trying to control them or even judge them.

This way of thinking, of "being," is appealing. We are, after all, mere human beings, unlike Dr. Manhattan, ignorant to most of the consequences of our actions. Who are we to judge others?

But then, doesn't judgment—the process of forming opinions, including critical opinions—have its benefits? Doesn't it motivate us to take action? If abolitionists did not condemn slavery, might it not have been institutionalized in the North, as well as the South? If civil rights activists did not rise up against Jim Crow, might we not still be living under the "separate but equal" doctrine? Isn't acceptance without judgment merely a way of maintaining the status quo, which may be far from just? Maybe it's better to have principles and live by them. Maybe accepting that which violates those principles is the last thing we ought to aspire to. This is one of several philosophical questions *Watchmen* takes up.

Rorschach has principles. They're good ones: Justice, fairness, honesty, possibly even decency. And he walks the walk. By the time the story reaches its climax, readers have little doubt that Rorschach is driven to do what he believes to be just and that he will stick by those principles to the end. Indeed, as we've already established, he is willing to kill for them.

Because *Watchmen* is not a typical superhero story, Rorschach's foil is not a typical villain. Adrian Veidt/Ozymandias wants to live in a peaceful, decent world, not one ravaged by crime and substance abuse and under constant threat of nuclear annihilation. He doesn't wish to rule such a world, just to live in it, not just for his own benefit, but for the benefit of humanity. And he too is willing to kill to get what he wants.

Part of *Watchmen*'s magic is that it makes you think you know whose vision you support and whose perspective you want to triumph, and then, like the Zen story at the beginning of this section, presents additional information that puts everything in a different perspective. At the end of the novel, you may still know whose vision you support and it may still be Rorschach's, but you're probably a little less sure. At the end of the story, Rorschach may still be right. But there is reason to doubt it, and there is no way to know for sure.

This lack of certainty creates a tension between acceptance and judgment, and years after reading the novel, it is this tension that I find myself contemplating again and again.

The best I seem able to do is to conclude that either extreme is flawed. It feels inhumane to accept without judgment that which is unjust. That's not the type of person I want to be. But neither do I want to delude myself into thinking that I have some special superpower (like Osterman's) to know how something will turn out... or even how something *has* turned out.

At the end of the story, despite the new information, Rorschach remains convinced that he knows what is best for the world. And though he may well be right, it is scary to me that he does not seem to even consider the possibility that he might not be. He can't. That type of cognitive process is decidedly gray, and as comics historian Bradford W. Wright described, Rorschach's worldview is "a set of black-and-white values that take many shapes but never mix into shades of gray, similar to the ink blot tests of his namesake."[19] I admire Rorschach's life journey. It took a lot of courage and integrity to survive his childhood and channel his experiences into something positive. I'm glad he survived and found a way to contribute to society. But I can't accept his worldview. Our reality is too complex to be easily dichotomized into good and evil, or even just and unjust. I think these are choices we do have to make, but I don't feel like I can truly trust someone who makes them without at least entertaining the possibility of being wrong.

Watchmen inspires social activism. It is filled with characters who want to change the world for the better. But, more than anything else, it inspires humility. If neither the smartest man in the world nor one with godlike powers to perceive time nonlinearly are in a position to confidently judge the story's deciding event, how can we ordinary humans portend to know anything with absolute certainty? Can a superhero story change the way you look at the world? It says something about both the story and our reality that the answer is: May be.

NOTES

1. It is worth noting that this line is often interpreted to impose a limitation on vengeance, not a minimum. That is, the Bible may well be instructing us to not be excessive in our vengeance, as in "only one eye for an eye, not more."
2. Oropeza, B. J. (2006). *The gospel according to superheroes: Religion and popular culture* (2nd ed.) New York: Lang.
3. They are punitive in the sense that justice is understood to occur when reasonable and proportionate punishment is applied to the offender, such that "the punishment fits the crime." This is also sometimes referred to as retributive justice. Additionally, our criminal justice system is also

punitive from the perspective of psychological behavioral theory, which posits that behaviors that are appropriately punished are less likely to occur in the future while those that are rewarded are more likely to be repeated.

4. Miller, F. (2002). *Batman: The Dark Knight returns* (hardcover edition). New York: DC Comics.
5. Eno, V., & El Csawza. (1988, May/June). Vincent Eno and El Csawza meet comics megastar Alan Moore. *Strange Things Are Happening*. Retrieved on October 29, 2011.
6. Skeem, J. L., Polaschek, D. L. L., Patrick, C. J., & Lilienfeld, S. O. (2011). Psychopathic personality: Bridging the gap between scientific evidence and public policy. *Psychological Science in the Public Interest, 12*(3), 95–162.
7. Fazel, S., & Danesh, J. (2002). Serious mental disorder in 23,000 prisoners: A systematic review of 62 surveys. *Lancet, 359*(9306), 545.
8. A few years after this shift to multiculturalism, writer and artist John Byrne introduced the first gay superhero, Northstar, although Marvel did not allow him to actually come out formally until 1992 (*Alpha Flight #106*). Despite restrictions imposed by the Comics Code Authority, other gay, lesbian, and bisexual characters followed, including long-time friends and lovers, Mystique and Destiny (*Uncanny X-men #265*). A list of gay and lesbian comic book characters is available athttp://www.gayleague.com/wordpress/characters/
9. Illinois Department of Transportation. (2009). Illinois Traffic Stop Report. Retrieved March 24, 2012, from http://www.dot.il.gov/travelstats/ITSS%202009%20Statewide%20and%20Agency%20Reports.pdf
10. Alexander, M. (2010). *The new Jim Crow: Mass incarceration in the age of colorblindness*. New York: New Press.
11. *X-Men* [Motion picture]. (2000). B. Toddman (Producer) & B. Singer (Director). United States: Twentieth Century Fox.
12. An earlier version of this section appeared in *Tikkun* magazine's January 2012 online edition: http://www.tikkun.org/nextgen/how-super-is-superhero-justice

13. In later stories and adaptations, including the 2002 movie, this phrase was modified to "With great power comes great responsibility."
14. Restorative practices actually come in many varied forms and differ considerably in the role that is given to the facilitator or circle-keeper and in the extent to which they involve the conflict community. Even so, restorative practices are much more likely to involve those impacted by the conflict than our formal justice systems.
15. "Restorative Circles" refers to a specific restorative practice developed in the favelas of Brazil by Dominic Barter and his associates. More information about this practice can be found at http://www.restorativecircles.org
16. Combination of the Indian words *Maha* (great) and *Metta* (loving-kindness, universal love).
17. I do not mean to suggest that all (or even most) violent crime is an attempt to punish others for the harm they caused. My purpose here is just to acknowledge that some violent crime does fall into this category. In this context, it is also worth stating that even when "offenders" pick random victims, they (the offenders) may still feel victimized by society and/or their life history (e.g., chronic physical abuse) and, in various intentional as well as unconscious ways, may be acting out of this felt sense of victimization.
18. An earlier version of this section was published on the author's *Psychology Today* blog, *Between the Lines*: http://www.psychologytoday.com/blog/between-the-lines/201001/the-zen-watchmen
19. Wright, B (2001). *Comic book nation: The transformation of youth culture in America*. Baltimore, MD: Johns Hopkins University Press, pp. 272–273.

Index